CONTENTS

THE FINANCIAL WELLBEING BOOK

CREATING FINANCIAL PEACE OF MIND

The Financial Wellbeing Book originally published in English by LID Business Media Limited

Reprinted and published in the English language by arrangement with LID Publishing

First Indian Edition, Published in 2023 by:
Embassy Book Distributors
120, Great Western Building, Maharashtra Chamber of Commerce Lane, Fort, Mumbai 400 023, India
Tel: (+9122) -30967415, 22819546
Email: info@embassybooks.in
www.embassybooks.in

ISBN: 978-81-19726-06-6

Cover and page design: Laura Hawkins
Printed & bound in India by Parksons Graphics Pvt. Ltd. Mumbai

THE FINANCIAL WELLBEING BOOK

CREATING FINANCIAL PEACE OF MIND

CHRIS BUDD

EBD

EMBASSY BOOKS
www.embassybooks.in

FOR OTHER TITLES IN THE SERIES...

CONCISE ADVICE LAB

SMALL BOOKS: BIG IDEAS

CLEVER CONTENT, DYNAMIC IDEAS, PRACTICAL SOLUTIONS AND ENGAGING VISUALS – A CATALYST TO INSPIRE NEW WAYS OF THINKING AND PROBLEM-SOLVING IN A COMPLEX WORLD

FOREWORD

Dr Catherine Zollman,
Clinical Lead Doctor of Penny Brohn UK

Penny Brohn UK is a pioneer in a whole-person approach to cancer, which is designed to support every aspect of a person's life.

Its unique approach acknowledges that cancer is more than just a physical event that happens in the body. Cancer affects the mind, body, spirit and emotions. It also impacts our relationships, community, environment and practical issues such as work and finances.

Penny Brohn helps people focus on each area of their lives and to make small but significant lifestyle changes to bring them into balance. Building resilience in this way supports our immune systems and the body's natural capacity to protect against cancer.

Stress inhibits this natural process and acts as a drain on the body's resources. Worries about money can be a major cause of stress, so achieving financial wellbeing is an important part of health.

Finding ways to reduce stress lies at the heart of Penny Brohn's whole-person approach.

The author is donating his proceeds from this book to Penny Brohn UK.

INTRODUCTION: **HOW THIS BOOK CAN INCREASE WELLBEING**

The underlying theme of this book is to encourage you to ignore the advice you find in books. That's not to say good advice cannot be found in books. But how do you know the advice given is appropriate for *you*?

KNOW THYSELF

In order to structure your finances in a way that is right for you, it is necessary to first decide what it is you want from your future. That's actually a lot harder than it may seem. There are many barriers to understanding the life you want; for example, not giving yourself the permission to be happy, facing financial limitations, or being overcommitted to others.

The key to financial wellbeing is not having the life others think you should have, but the life you want.

Now repeat after me:
We are *all* individual; and
We are *all* unique.

If you just said those lines out loud, you really need this book! And you are on your way to financial wellbeing.

WELLBEING

The research institute Gallup[1] conducted more than two million interviews with people around the world about wellbeing. Their findings conclude that wellbeing can be split into five components:

- Career wellbeing
- Social wellbeing
- Financial wellbeing
- Physical wellbeing
- Community wellbeing

Although this book is primarily focused on financial wellbeing, it is necessary to take into account how your personalised version of financial wellbeing interacts with the other areas of wellbeing. For example, someone focused entirely on the accumulation of wealth may not have very strong social wellbeing.

FINANCIAL WELLBEING

Financial wellbeing can also be broken down into five elements[2]:

- A clear path to achieve identifiable objectives;
- Control of daily finances;
- The ability to cope with a financial shock;
- Financial options in life; and
- Clarity and security for those we leave behind.

We will at look each of these elements in turn, underpinned by the importance of "know thyself". This will create the space for decisions to be made and will ensure those decisions are the right ones for you.

HOW THE BOOK WORKS

A good financial plan will follow a simple process:

STEP 1 Understand your objectives and motivations in life ("know thyself")
STEP 2 Create a realistic financial plan that helps achieve those objectives and motivations
STEP 3 Monitor and review regularly

We will consider each of the five elements that contribute to financial wellbeing and then turn these into a financial plan.

More resources are available from the website **www.financialwell-being.co.uk**

Sprinkled liberally throughout the book are practical tips to help you manage finances and achieve financial wellbeing for a happier and healthier life. Anecdotes are widely used to illustrate the various points being made. Accordingly, with this first anecdote it is easy to demonstrate why this book is so important.

THE ONE ABOUT THE MUZZY HEAD

Chris had set up his business 12 years previously. Things were going well now, but it had been a hard journey and at times very stressful. Recently Chris had been suffering from what his doctor called a 'muzzy head' and was finding it difficult to concentrate.

Chris's doctor suggested they take some blood tests. When the results came in, the doctor gave the good news. The results had come back all clear. There was nothing wrong. The doctor rose to show Chris out of the door.

Except there was still something wrong. Chris still had the muzzy head. He told his doctor that he had done a bit of his own research that suggested it might be stress or depression. The doctor gave Chris a rather tatty, photocopied piece of paper entitled "Depression Questionnaire" and told him to come back in two weeks' time with the completed questionnaire.

When Chris got home, he sat down with the form. The first question was, "How many times a week do you feel like killing yourself?"

Chris didn't complete the questionnaire or go back to the doctor. Coincidentally, a friend was training to be a business coach and asked Chris to be a guinea pig for her. The three coaching sessions she gave Chris enabled him to gain clarity and understand what he wanted from his life and his business.

Implementing changes to his business meant Chris gave other members of the team more responsibility. He was then able to focus on doing the things he enjoyed. He made a big decision to take Wednesdays off and use that time to resurrect his dream of writing novels.

A year later, he no longer suffered from the muzzy head feeling. Two years further on, he published his first novel.

This is a true story. I was that Chris.

PART ONE

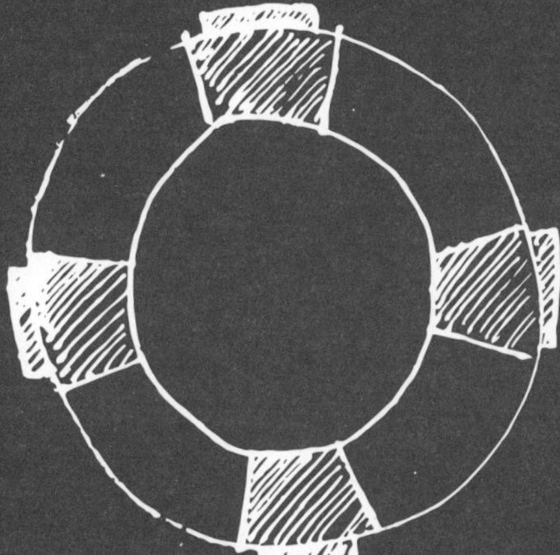

IDENTIFIABLE OBJECTIVES

The first area of financial wellbeing is:

1. A clear path to identifiable objectives

People who have high levels of financial wellbeing tend to have income levels sufficient for their needs. They have a standard of living with which they are satisfied. This is not the same as being wealthy. *It is being content with what you have.* It is aligning your lifestyle with your finances. It is about having enough for the life you want.

Therefore, the first step is to identify our objectives.

DECIDE ON THE DESTINATION

UNIQUELY YOU

Having picked up this book, you might be wanting to get into the numbers that influence your life financially. You are probably keen to map out your future so that you can start to make decisions and changes in your life for the better. Before we get specific, however, I'd like to encourage you to take the time to think about where you're headed. In fact, take quite a few moments – because this is actually the most important part of the process.

What you want from your life is unique to you. No one else can answer this question. You should take some time to work out what you want your financial plan to achieve and how it can be used to generate maximum wellbeing.

THE ONE ABOUT CHOOSING BREAD

In my second year at university I shared a house with three others in Levenshulme, Manchester. Like many people sharing for the first time, we idealistically thought we would rotate the cooking and cleaning duties between us.

Off we went to the local supermarket together to do a communal shop. The first section that greeted us was bread. I headed straight to the white, medium-sliced bread. Andy went to the white, thick-sliced bread. Julie went to the granary medium-sliced and Jane to the wholemeal unsliced. We all stood in a row, looking at each other, bewildered, as if to say, "What are you doing? That's not bread. *This* is bread."

Needless to say, the produce section (bypassed by me and Andy) and turkey burgers (which Andy bought in bulk) were even more divisive. We quickly realised that no one solution was going to fit all four of us and for the next two years we mostly prepared our own meals.

If you are confident that you know where you want your life to go and have everything sorted, skip to Part 2. But I would suggest that to do so would be like taking a bunch of ingredients and throwing them in a pot without having any idea what it is you are trying to cook.

WHAT DOES YOUR FUTURE LOOK LIKE?

In order to create a plan, you need to know what it is you want to achieve. An old Chinese proverb says, "Every long journey starts with a small step." First, however, we must ensure that we are about to start walking in the right direction.

For the *individual,* this means understanding your own motivations and objectives in life. Only then can you create a financial plan that helps you get there.

For a *business owner,* this means creating a business plan that gets your business to where you want it to be. You need to know what you want from your business.

For the *elderly or someone with a life-threatening illness,* this may take the form of getting your affairs in order, making sure that your nearest and dearest are cared for and not left with decisions to make after your passing.

Spend some time deciding on the destination, and consider the motivation behind your choice of goals and objectives to make sure you are aiming for the right ones.

TIP: Write down the numbers one through ten on a piece of paper. Starting with one, write down five things you like to do that make you happy. Next, from numbers six to ten, write down anything that you would like to do but currently don't do, for whatever reason. There is no limit, but four or five would be plenty to work with.

You now have the beginnings of a plan. The next step is to test and challenge this.

WHOSE GOALS ARE THESE?

Do we really understand our motivations for establishing these goals? How can we be sure the goals we have chosen will bring us wellbeing and happiness? To what extent are our objectives defined by others, by our parents and peers, by our own need for permission? (See "How Can I Generate More Options?" later in this section.)

THE ONE ABOUT CHARLOTTE AND GOLF

Charlotte was a relatively wealthy lady, the sort of wealth accumulated from a lifetime of hard work. She was still working as a management consultant at the age of 63 and enjoyed her job, especially the feeling of making a difference. For several years we had been trying to persuade Charlotte to spend some of the money she earned rather than continuing to save. She would always answer that they didn't have enough money to waste and that her father had instilled in her a sensible approach to money.

Her husband had recently retired and wanted her to take some time off. During a meeting, we asked what they might do with a bit more free time. They both played golf and also liked the idea of travel, but Charlotte was insistent that they couldn't afford to do anything too expensive.

We went through their financial plan and demonstrated that they could spend a lot more on travel and still have enough set aside for the rest of their lives. Charlotte, sitting on our meeting-room sofa with her arms crossed, was not convinced, despite the proof in front of her. We changed the subject and gave her a little time to absorb what she had seen. We talked about golf. We wondered how much it would cost them to go to the next Ryder Cup with VIP passes. Charlotte's ears pricked up. We suggested calling a company we deal with that organises such trips, just to get an idea of price. As I left the room to make the telephone call, I turned to Charlotte to confirm. "So I'm asking for an idea of cost for two VIP tickets to the Ryder Cup, ok?"

"Yes," said Charlotte. She then paused for a moment, before adding excitedly, "In America!"

By the time you have finished reading this book I hope you will have a greater understanding of what you want your life to look like. You should also have a pretty good idea of what you need to do to get there in the form of a financial plan – which we will get to shortly.

> **TIP:** Exploring the future requires time – real time, and almost certainly help from others. Who else will your financial plan affect? Talk to them, but also to someone not affected, someone independent.

GET SOME HELP

In thinking about the future and what it might hold, it is important to challenge your assumptions and dare to dream. Any consideration as to what happiness and wellbeing mean to you will benefit from a fresh look.

WHY WE CANNOT CHALLENGE OURSELVES

Have you ever had a debate with someone and simply could not understand how your opponent could hold the view he or she does? Chances are they felt the same way about you.

From the moment we are born, we go through a cycle over and over again. We have an experience, which shapes our view of something, which in turn creates values, which influences our actions, which creates new experiences.

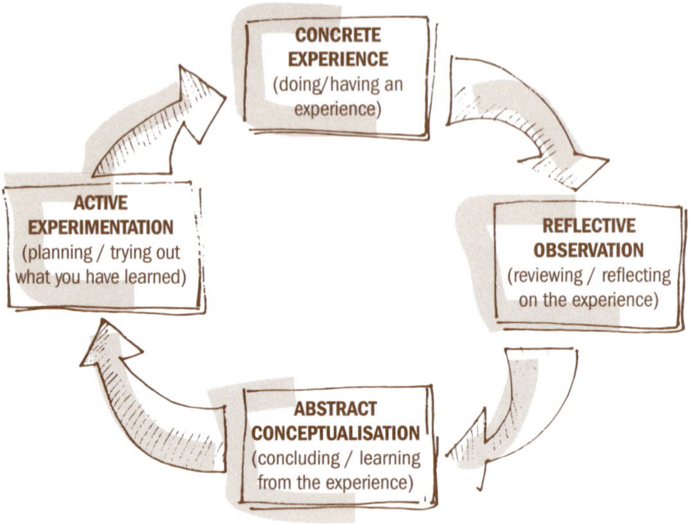

Diagram: Kolb's Learning Cycle[3]

This process never ends. However, the experiences we create for ourselves often confirm our values, rather than challenge them. With our experiences we tend to reinforce our values, which is why we cannot challenge ourselves.

"A DOCTOR WHO OPERATES ON HIMSELF HAS A FOOL FOR A PATIENT" **(RICHARD HUDSON)**

This creates a dilemma. If our view of the world is shaped by our experiences, then how can we give advice to one another? We often seek advice from someone who is more knowledgeable or more experienced in a particular subject matter, which makes the advice valuable. But the knowledge and/or experience of advisors on a particular subject matter will have been defined, at least in part, by their view of the world. It will have been shaped by thousands of small experiences that have built their personality. Their advice will be affected by their history of experiences. Their advice will therefore come from a personal viewpoint which may make no difference, some difference, or all the difference in the world.

THE ONE ABOUT ASSUMPTIONS

During my training as a business coach, I met a new coachee for the first time. Gilbert was married, with five children, and was working very hard in the business, six days a week and often Sunday mornings too. He wanted to form a management structure to ease the burden on him. As we talked, I started to wonder what his life must be like, how his children felt not seeing their father. I could see the direction our coaching sessions were likely to take and the positive effect they might have on his life.

After a while I tried to summarise our conversation so far, what I had learnt about his business and his world view. I saved the best until last. "And as a result of the changes you'd like to implement, you will regain control of your life, and be able to spend more time with your children."

"Where did you get that idea from?" Gilbert replied. "I'm quite happy with how much I see my kids, thank you. I want to create time so that I can expand the business."

I had made the mistake of applying my own world view to Gilbert's situation. Coaching someone with very different values to your own is one of the challenging – and interesting – aspects of being a business coach.

COACH, MENTOR, OR FRIEND?

To get a better understanding of your objectives and work out what you want from your future, you may find it helpful to work with a coach or a mentor. But how should you choose?

In fairly simple terms, the difference between coaches (business coach or life coach) and mentors is that coaches will help you work out the answers to your questions yourself, whereas mentors will have experience and answers and can therefore tell you what they think you should do. Both methods can be beneficial, but it is important to know which you are receiving.

Coaches will tend to be a fairly short-term appointment. The objective of coaching is for coachees to develop themselves to the point that they no longer need the coach. Mentors will tend to be more long term. The advice they dispense can be addictive and a mentee may come to rely on having the advice of the mentor at hand.

Both have their place. Both can enhance wellbeing.

Coaching can help individuals understand themselves better, to learn and develop, to better understand their place in an organisation, in society, among their friends, and in their own lives. Mentoring allows individuals to use the experience of others, and to obtain solutions to problems that they may not have encountered before from someone who has.

But both have pitfalls, too. Coaching doesn't work too well if all you really want is an answer to a problem. A two-hour coaching session can be frustrating when coachees just want someone to tell them what to do. Advice from a mentor may be tainted by the mentor's own world view. Successful business people can sometimes forget the significant part that luck played in their journey. What worked for them may not work for you.

Perhaps friends have asked you for help, either for just a friendly ear or more specific advice. Take a moment to consider whether the advice is based upon your world view, or theirs.

TIP: A challenge

When dispensing advice, it is important to first understand the problem. Most of us jump in with our opinion far too early, before we've really understood the issue. To test just how good you are at really listening, try this challenge.

Pick someone, perhaps a friend or work colleague. Someone you know, but not really well. Now, ask a question about him or her. It might be "What would you do if you won the lottery?" Or maybe, "If you could change one thing about work, what would it be?".

Your challenge is to see how long you can keep the conversation going, obeying these three simple rules:

- You are only allowed to ask questions
- You are not allowed to express an opinion
- You are not allowed to mention yourself.

See how long you can talk together without breaking one of these rules. Try it with a few people. You will start to find that not only will you learn an awful lot more about the people around you, but that they start to learn more about themselves.

The advice one receives from friends may well fall into all of the traps outlined above.

WELL-MEANING ADVICE

Most financial advisers have a story about a client who did something daft on the basis of advice from "the man down the pub." The advice may have been well intended, but it was ill informed and did not take into account the client's circumstances. When seeking to better understand what you want from your future, it is important to speak to people who will give you impartial, knowledgeable advice – not advice based upon what they would do. This type of advice may well be suitable for them and their circumstances, but it may not suit yours.

THE ONE ABOUT THE SECRETARIES OF JULIET BLOG

Shakespeare's play, *Romeo and Juliet*, was set in Verona, Italy. If you go to Verona you can visit the actual balcony from the play, the famous location of one of the most famous scenes in literature. Here it is:

It is quite amazing to stand underneath this balcony and imagine being there when Juliet so famously called for her beloved Romeo. It's such a powerful experience that hundreds of thousands of people visit the balcony every year. The walls are covered with graffiti, most of it addressed to Romeo and Juliet. One can only imagine what the young lovers would actually think of it all. Many people take things one step farther. Around 10,000 people a year – most, but not all, women – write letters to Juliet asking for her advice, each of them expecting a response.

So, just to recap: around 500,000 people a year visit a balcony on the side of a house. And 10,000 people a year write letters –

to a fictional character, who, even if she was not fictional, would have lived more than 500 years ago. A young woman who (spoiler alert) kills herself at the end of the play.

A group of women in Verona who call themselves "The Secretaries of Juliet" respond to these letters, as Juliet. Many of the letters can be heart-breaking, even when you remember that they are written to a fictional character and the authors expect a response. Most importantly, The Secretaries of Juliet take great care never to give advice, but instead urge the lovelorn correspondents to search within their hearts, to stay true to themselves or, if more practical advice is required, to speak to those they love and respect for advice.

Always positive, always caring, but never prescriptive.

Let us now look at some key questions that need to be considered.

HOW MUCH IS ENOUGH?

Look again at the list of things that make you happy. How can you be sure the list is right, that you have chosen the right destination for you? It is imperative for you to take the time to understand what you want from life. Once you have a good understanding of this, you will be better placed to answer the crucial question: **How much is enough?**

The answer to this question will be different for everyone. It is essential that you know what your answer is. It might be a number, but it is more likely to be an ideal. As with all planning, it is the time spent considering the answers that provides the value, not necessarily the answer itself. Clarity brings wellbeing.

CAN MONEY MAKE YOU HAPPY?

Wellbeing comes from financial security. This will be different for everyone and is not necessarily dependent on being wealthy. For some, the pursuit of money seems to be a life goal. For others, money seems to have no relevance other than to put food on the table. In truth, most of us are somewhere in between – but do we really understand our relationship to wealth? How does wealth contribute to wellbeing?

Many will assert that money does not make you happy. This is clearly absurd – just ask someone who has received a bonus from work and can now afford a holiday.

It is fair to say that money does not bring happiness on its own. Surveys have shown that the ongoing accumulation of money for its own sake does not further wellbeing. So, more specifically, it should be said that having enough money to do what you want creates happiness.

THE ONE ABOUT THE SURVEY

In 1978, researchers in America[4] studied 22 major lottery winners and 29 paralysed accident victims. They sought to answer the question of whether happiness is relative to circumstance.

Theories have been put forth to suggest that wealth does not lead to wellbeing. The Hedonic Treadmill theory, for example, suggests that humans will revert to a stable level of happiness individual to them, irrespective of life events. In the research, the two different groups were asked if they were happy before their life-changing event, and if they were happy after.

It might be expected that the lottery winners were happier and the accident victims less. It might even be considered that the lottery winners were less happy. In fact, the results were even more interesting. The people from either group who said they were happy before their event said they were happy after (given a period of adjustment). Those who were unhappy before were unhappy after. The study went on to provide some reasons for this, such as the increased pleasure the paralysed accident victims took from mundane events. However, the conclusion from the study is that our level of happiness is relatively unchanged by dramatic life events.

In order for wealth to create wellbeing we need:

- To know what we want
- To have clear objectives
- To understand our motivations.

HOW CAN I GENERATE MORE OPTIONS?

It can be difficult to think of new ideas and generate new options for the future. One reason for this is self-limiting beliefs. Everyone's world view is made up of their collected experiences and their reactions to them. These create values, which influence experiences, and create new reactions. And around the cycle we go from the moment we are born. This creates a belief system that inevitably informs our choices and options. These very beliefs, however, may in fact be limiting our options.

Here are a few examples of self-limiting beliefs:

- I can't do X because of Y
- I won't be happy until I have enough money
- I don't have enough money (a tactic to give ourselves permission to remain stuck)
- I have too many responsibilities to have fun
- Earning money is hard work
- I'm expected to ... (by whom?)
- It's just the way things are (collective assumption)
- Options only increase with wealth.

The key point here is that beliefs are not truths.

It is easy to get caught up in allowing our beliefs to define us. They shape our thinking and our actions, but can prevent us from seeing opportunities and can discourage us from even trying at all.

It is difficult to change one's beliefs and fixed ideas. There is frequently a time lag between changes in thinking and actual changes in our emotional state. Even when we recognise that something isn't logical or rational, there will be an internal forceful debate between our rational and irrational thoughts over a period of time.

The process of generating more options is really about being creative, using lateral thinking to break out from the limitations of the current world view.

TIP: Here are a few ideas when trying to generate new options:

- Use open questions to explore more ideas: "What else ..."
- Use brainstorming – the process of creating ideas without limitations and without judgment
- Get all the ideas out before considering their merits
- Use questions that suspend limit-based thinking: "If there were no limits on ... what would you do then?"
- Use questions that break the rules: "What if you didn't need to ..."

You are aiming to create and list as many options as possible with as little evaluation or judgment as possible. Only after such a list is created should you evaluate the ideas for suitability and feasibility.

And if you dismiss an idea, test whether this is because it contradicts one of your self-limiting beliefs.

BE SPECIFIC

In order to gain real clarity over what you want your future to look like, ask yourself a few simple questions:

- If you no longer needed to work, what would you do with your day?
- What are your basic requirements, what are the "nice to haves," and what would you like to do in your dreams?
- If money were no object, what would you do with your time?
- Is there anything you really want to do that you never have done?

Dare to dream. Go on. Try to imagine the future in daily terms. How would you like to spend your time? Of course, this will be somewhat circular. You may dream of a life that is out of reach. Actually the opposite is often the case – many people envisage a life constrained by what they think they can afford.

So be sensible. What are the things that would make you happy?

TIP: Take the list of things that make you happy – hopefully by now you have reconsidered and updated these – and rate each one according to how important it is to you, from one to ten. Next, rate each one by how much you currently enjoy it, from one to ten.

You should now be looking at a prioritised list!

CONCLUSION

By the end of this section you should have identified your objectives. The next step is to add detail for these dreams and plot a path to turn them into reality.

PART TWO

A CLEAR PATH

ARE YOU READY?

By the end of Part One (or if you skipped straight to here) you should have a pretty good idea of what you want your future to look like. This has to be the right future for you, for your family, and for those you will one day leave behind.

If you don't have a clear idea, there may be two reasons:

- You haven't spent enough time in Part One
- You need to put some numbers together with your ideas to find out how realistic they are.

If it is the first reason, I'd suggest you go back and spend more time on Part One, and maybe enlist some independent help. Carry on working through the book, by all means, to get a framework ready. But until you have real clarity from Part One, the rest of the process has no foundation upon which to build.

Once you have clarity about your future, you can move on to add some detail!

WHAT DO YOU SPEND? THE GRUNT WORK

Now that we've got clarity over the future we can try to get clarity over today.

To continue the house building analogy, we are going to build the frame of the house on top of the foundations we laid down in Part One. The foundations make sure the house won't fall down. The structure determines the size and shape of the house.

This will take a little time, but it really is worth it. You need to spend some time analysing how you spend your money. Make a cuppa or pour a glass of wine and go through your last six months' bank statements. Summarise how much you spend in different categories. There are apps which help you do this in a simple way.

Financial planners have software for this sort of thing which can take into account all sorts of variations and scenarios. If you don't want to engage an adviser then a simple spreadsheet can give a reasonable indication, but do be careful – once you get into the detail of this, it can suck up your time!

Given that our objective in this book is to increase wellbeing and reduce stress, it would seem logical to avoid one of the things we hate the most; it would make sense to take advantage of it.

THE ONE ABOUT SPENDING TIME WITH THE KIDS

Jon works for an accounting firm. He came to us for advice on a number of fronts, including his pension and investment portfolio. As with all clients, we started off by asking some searching questions around how he saw his future. After a few meetings with Jon and then (at our insistence) with his wife, a picture of their ideal future began to emerge. It involved Jon not working such long hours, fewer nights spent away from home, and more time spent with his wife and young daughter. We agreed that a cash-flow forecast would be a good idea to put some numbers on this vision of the future. We sent Jon a spreadsheet of income and expenditure to complete so that we could plug the numbers into our system and see what the future might look like. It never came back.

A month later and we again called Jon to ask for the spreadsheet. "It's ok," he said, telling us that he'd done the forecasting himself, thereby saving our fee. We asked for a copy. He had, indeed, done it himself, and pretty well too. There were a few assumptions we challenged and a few tweaks here and there, but overall he'd done a reasonable job. Knowing how complex this could be, we asked how long this had taken him. "Two nights, from 6 pm until midnight, and most of Saturday," he replied, with a little pride in his voice.

We pointed out that one of his objectives was to spend more time with his family, and yet he'd just spent two whole nights and half a weekend in a room on his own.

There is no shortcut to this process, and the work you do here will be used again later. So settle down over your bank statements and start summarising where all your money goes!

Here's a list of typical items that you should consider. This is not exhaustive; add any category that that you spend money on.

REGULAR BILLS	**SHOPPING**	**CARS**	**LEISURE**
MORTGAGE/RENT	CLOTHING	PETROL/DIESEL	HOLIDAYS
COUNCIL TAX	WINES/ BEER	SERVICING AND MAINTENANCE	SPORTS/ HOBBIES
WATER	BEAUTY	CAR INSURANCE	ENTERTAINMENT

ELECTRICITY	TRANSPORT	CAR OTHER	EATING OUT
GAS	CHILDCARE		CASH WITHDRAWALS
BROADBAND			
TELEPHONE			
HOME INSURANCE/ CONTENTS			
PRIVATE MEDICAL INSURANCE			
LIFE ASSURANCE			
FOOD AND HOUSEKEEPING			
PROPERTY MAINTENANCE			
SCHOOL FEES			
SUBSCRIPTIONS			
PETS			
SAVINGS			

TIP: If you have to make assumptions on expenditure, it is advisable to add 20% to the value. As with a business plan, people tend to underestimate their costs and overestimate their income! We especially underestimate the cost of luxury items—products or experiences that are not essential or necessary, but make life more pleasant.

CREATING THE PLAN - CASH FLOW MODELLING

To create a financial forecast, you will need the following information:

- The income and expenditure summary you have just completed
- Likely changes to income and expenditure in the future
- One-off expenditure (e.g., weddings, car replacement)
- One-off payments received (e.g., inheritance)
- Current assets and liabilities.

Some of these might be easy to find, such as cash in the bank, but others less so – old pension schemes, for example.

Some assumptions will be needed. These will be informed by the results from Part One. When will you retire and therefore cease receiving earned income? Will you work part time, or perhaps move into consultancy?

TIP: Be careful about assuming too much in terms of inheritance. Care-home fees, in particular, can rapidly eat away people's accumulated wealth in their final years.

This exercise is designed to answer that one simple question: **If I live the life I want, when will the money run out?**

CASH-FLOW FORECAST NUMBER 1– KEEPING IT SIMPLE

The next stage is to create a spreadsheet that will produce a summary of your income and expenditure not only today but for every year for the rest of your life.

Our spreadsheet should have nine columns. We will fill it in as we go along. We can then analyse what this first forecast tells you.

TIP: A comprehensive case study, including downloadable spreadsheets, is available from www.financialwell-being.co.uk. It features Mr and Mrs Procter, who are in their 50s. This section may be more meaningful if you take a look at the case study.

The first column will contain your age as it progresses over the years; let's take it up to age 100. The second to the ninth column should have the following headings, in order:

2. Expenditure
3. Income from employment, then state pension
4. Income shortfall or surplus
5. Assets for income (Pensions, ISAs, etc.)
6. Debt
7. Non-income assets, (Main residence, etc.)
8. One-off expenditure
9. One-off receipts.

Consider and make a list for each of the following; some examples have been given for guidance.

EXPENDITURE:

- This is the expenditure summary
- Include financially dependent children and the costs associated so that in later years this can be removed
- Consider when nursing home fees arrive.

INCOME:

- Pay, including increases through promotions and any possible bonuses
- Expected start of state pensions
- Income from assets in the future (to come from the "Assets for Income" column).

INCOME SHORTFALL OR SURPLUS:

- This will be a formula of income minus expenditure
- This number will either be added or deducted from the assets column.

ASSETS FOR INCOME:

- Pension fund and savings/investments.

DEBT:

- Mortgage
- Future purchases that require debt, such as a new car
- Any other debts, such as personal and credit cards.

NON-INCOME ASSETS:

- Main residence
- Holiday home
- Anything else you might be able to sell later in life.

ONE-OFF EXPENDITURE:

- This might include weddings or that dream trip.

ONE-OFF RECEIPTS:

- Include any expected inheritance (but be realistic).

Now, start filling the spreadsheet in. We're ignoring growth and inflation for the moment, so some columns will remain the same over the years (such as your house price), while others will change (such as your income when you retire).

LESSONS

In the case study, Mr and Mrs Procter run out of money. We'll look at what we might change in a moment, but first let's draw some early conclusions, a few things to ponder. **Remember the objective: we are looking to enhance financial wellbeing by creating a clear path to our identifiable objectives.**

THE IMPORTANCE OF YOUR ASSETS

The important column is "Assets for Income". This is the one to keep an eye on, because this is where the income is going to come from when you are no longer earning a regular pay check. Therefore, it's also the one to add to as much as possible when you are earning.

If you are showing no regular savings we are in a "We've got no spare cash at the moment" situation, not uncommon with clients when we first meet them. **The forecast has therefore identified a problem**. The action point may well be to investigate current expenditure further in order to find some spare cash that could be added to your savings.

DARE TO DREAM

This forecast should show a steady few years, perhaps up until your retirement. This is the point in life where there may be a decrease in income but where expenditure remains the same. If no changes are made, there might not be any significant excess available for dream fulfilment, such as travel (which tends to be the number-one choice of luxury in retirement). This is not exactly the cash flow for designing your ideal life, but it is a pragmatic forecast.

UNDERSTAND THE VALUE OF YOUR ASSETS

Some assets in your forecast might be very difficult to value; art or shares in a business are good examples. The value of such items are often very different for someone buying them than for the person selling them. A cash-flow forecast can be used in such instances to answer the question of how much the asset *needs* to be sold for, rather than how much it might be worth.

THE ONE ABOUT HOW MUCH THE BUSINESS WAS WORTH

Ella had been running her own fashion design business for 15 years. Now 62, she was tired and stressed and wanted to move on. The business had been successful and she had used the profits wisely. We had helped her build up a sizeable pension and ISA portfolio, plus she owned a property in Devon. Her plan was to sell the business and her house, then retire to Devon. She and her husband lived modestly.

The accountant valued the business at £500,000 and so she instructed them to find a buyer. Interest was sparse, but eventually a realistic offer came to buy the business for £300,000. Ella was set to turn down the offer. When asked her reasons, she said that the business was worth £500,000. After 17 years of hard work, she didn't want to sell the business on the cheap. But, we countered, you would have all the money you need to fulfil your objectives and motivations. "Yes," replied Ella, "but I built this business from scratch. I don't want to let someone have it for almost half of what it is worth."

But, we persisted, she didn't need that extra money. Her objective was to retire to Devon, and this offer would help her achieve that objective. Ella turned down the offer. She eventually sold the business two years later for £400,000. Sadly, she then retired to Devon and suffered a nervous breakdown.

LATER LIFE

It is important to consider expenses that will be incurred later in life, such as the costs of moving into a retirement home. It may be necessary to sell valuable assets, such as your home, to fund this. In the full spreadsheet (available from the website), the assets get a boost when Mr and Mrs Procter move into a retirement home. The house was sold, and could be used to pay the care-home fees. Care homes can be extremely costly, and the assumption of £60k per annum for two people is by no means extravagant.

LEAVING SOMETHING FOR THE KIDS

One area in which we find a huge range of opinion is that of inheritance. For some people, leaving something for their children is the major focus of their financial planning. Others take the attitude that the kids can make their own way, and plan how they can make the last penny drop out of their bank account just as the life support machine gets turned off! It is important to build whichever approach you choose into your forecast. It would be a shame to make sacrifices to your lifestyle only to end up with a large amount left at the end that is more than your children might want or need.

YOUR CHALLENGE

Since running out of money is not an option for your forecast, the ultimate conclusion to this exercise is that if this appears to be the case, you will need to make changes to ensure that your money does not run out.

Let's take a look at the variables and consider what you might want to change. In this way we can develop the forecast into something that will be more suitable to you and at the same time something that is achievable.

ASSUMPTIONS

In the first model we have made no assumptions for assets or liabilities increasing, be it costs (inflation), wages, investments, and so on. In practice, different types of costs, debts, and assets rise or fall at different rates. The interplay between these can be crucial to the accuracy of your forecast.

DIFFERENT ASSET CLASSES

At this point, an explanation of financial jargon is required. The term "asset class" refers to different types of investments, such as property, cash, and shares in the stock market. There are many subdivisions (residential and commercial property, for example, or shares in UK or Japan or USA). Each of these different asset classes behaves in a different way under the influence of external factors. The market forces that affect residential property, for example, are very different than those affecting commercial property. We are going to make very simplistic assumptions on growth, so it's important to be aware that the reality is far more complicated.

CASH-FLOW FORECAST NUMBER 2 – THE EFFECT OF INVESTMENT GROWTH

The next step is to decide what assumptions you are going to use. Just a small change (increase or decrease) in the real rate of return of investments (the annual rate of growth above inflation) can make a huge difference over a 30-year timescale. First of all, let's keep everything the same but assume that your investments grow at 2% above inflation each year with no other changes. This actually doesn't mean that investments grow at 2%, but that the investments need to grow 2% quicker than inflation – the "real rate of return."

Let's go back to Mr and Mrs Procter. With no growth, their assets ran out at age 75. If we add just 2% real growth per annum the assets run out at age 80, at which point they sell the house and use the money to fund the care-home fees. This forecast can be seen on the second spreadsheet, available on the website.

CONCLUSION

Since we have not changed anything else, we can see that achieving an extra 2% growth per annum on our investments dramatically changes our financial future. So how do we achieve extra returns on our assets? By taking investment risk. Risk tolerance and capacity for loss are key considerations in creating a financial plan and understanding yourself. For this reason we will look into these in much more detail in Part Four.

FINANCIAL PLANNING VARIABLES

We've touched on the effect changes to asset classes of an investment portfolio, growth assumptions, and level of investment risk can have. Let's now consider a couple of other assumptions that we can change.

DOWNSIZING. For many people, repayment of a mortgage has been the main focus of their retirement planning. Upon reaching retirement age, they realise that they have insufficient income and yet live in a house bigger than they need after the kids have left home. Moving to a smaller house and releasing the capital to provide income is a common solution.

INHERITANCE. We've mentioned already the danger of overestimating potential inheritance. So why not find out? It is not uncommon to discover that elderly relatives have been living frugally to try to leave as much money as possible to their adult children, when the children would have preferred for the parents to have enjoyed their lives a bit more. A discussion with parents about inheritance might feel awkward, but it will make planning a great deal more meaningful.

CASH-FLOW FORECAST NUMBER 3 – MODELLING DIFFERENT SCENARIOS

So far we have taken the following steps:

1. Thought long and hard about what we want out of life
2. Set realistic objectives for the future
3. Set up a financial forecast based upon current circumstances to achieve those objectives in the future
4. Added in a modest growth assumption to the investments
5. Considered changes that can be made and observe the possible effect of these on the future.

The next step is to change the future – to model different scenarios and find out what might be achievable and perhaps discover what sacrifices should be taken now to lead to a better future. This is the fun part. This is where you sit back and think, "I wonder if I could ..."

WHAT ARE THE COMMON SCENARIOS?

If you're struggling to think of anything you'd like to change about your future, you might want to revisit Part One. Daring to dream is a big part of financial planning. To help you on your way, here is a list of some of the most typical questions that people ask about their cash flow forecast:

- Can I retire early?
- How much can we afford to give to our children and still be ok ourselves?
- Can I repay my mortgage early?
- How should I structure my will? (Model how much needs to be left to a surviving spouse and therefore how much can be handed down or given away)
- When should I consider care homes and what quality could they be?
- What do I actually want to do—and therefore spend—in my retirement?
- What would be the impact of a possible divorce settlement? (Cash flow modelling can be a useful tool for agreeing divorce settlements.)

Let's take the most common request: "Can I retire early?" We can build on the second forecast, but this time, retiring three years earlier, you will need to remove three years of income. This has been performed on the website example and the updated forecast shows Mr and Mrs Procter retiring at 62. Receiving three years less of their income, their money runs out at 68 but gets topped up once, when they reach 70, by an inheritance, and again when the house is sold. This forecast might suggest that early retirement is not possible. But if they make a few sacrifices now, this may allow the couple to retire three years early if they really are keen to do so.

How can you make up a shortfall to achieve an earlier retirement? First, you can increase the growth assumption to 3%. To reiterate, that means our invested money needs to grow at 3% above inflation every year, after any charges. Alternatively, the promise of early retirement may be sufficient to inspire a few lifestyle changes now to increase the ability to save.

In our case study, after a chat, Mr and Mrs Procter decided that they could forgo a few things now in order to increase their savings. A further, final change they agreed to was downsizing a little earlier than they had planned, moving to a smaller house at age 68 rather than wait until they were forced to. In fact they thought they would like to rent a flat in the middle of town. This gave them the value of the house to invest for income, but did mean they had the cost of renting the flat to add to their expenditure.

THE ONE ABOUT MORTALITY AND RETIREMENT

An actuarial study[5] of pension payments from the retirement funds of large corporations, such as Boeing Aerospace, showed that a person who retired at the age of 55 had a typical life expectancy of 83. A person retiring at 65, however, had a life expectancy of 67.

They concluded that for every year we work after the age of 55, we lose two years of our life expectancy. They further observed that those who retired at 55 were not necessarily using their time idly. They often continued to work part time or at things they wanted to do but which might be lower paid.

By making a series of relatively small decisions, you can hone in on a plan that could give you a very different financial future than you had thought possible. Retirement can happen years earlier but you will need to accept a higher level of investment risk – accepting short-term volatility in the hope of higher longer-term returns – than you may have originally been comfortable with. Whether these are things you are willing to accept, and whether it is consistent with your capacity for financial loss, are issues that you will need to consider very carefully. There will be more on this subject in Part Four.

In the case of Mr and Mrs Procter, they started to really understand their joint priorities in life. For them it was important to spend time together, and they were willing to make some small sacrifices in order to achieve this.

As you have noted, there are many other things you can change to project a more positive financial forecast. For example, rather than retire fully, you may be able to work part time or move into working as a self-employed consultant for a few years. This will retain a level of income while enjoying greater flexibility of your time.

REVIEW AND MONITOR

Once you have prepared your forecast and you are happy with its potential outcome, all that remains is for you to make sure it becomes a reality! This involves keeping an eye on all of your investments and how they are performing. It requires you to change the forecast as circumstances change (perhaps that inheritance from Auntie Mabel comes in after all, or maybe the kids get good jobs quicker than expected).

A cash-flow forecast is based on a series of assumptions about the future. It's almost impossible that these will all turn out to be correct, so you should only view the forecast you have prepared as a guide. It is also important that you review your forecast from time to time, at least annually.

TIP: Once you have created your personal forecast, make sure you spend the time to regularly review and update it.

The review is possibly the most important part in the process of financial planning. A meeting with your financial adviser, who tells you things are going better than expected, is wonderful. But a meeting with your financial adviser who tells you things aren't going so well means you need to make essential changes.

CONCLUSION

Having completed these first two sections, you should have a better understanding of your future and you should now be able to create a clear path to achieving that future. We have completed the first component of financial wellbeing: To have a clear path to achieve identifiable objectives. However, it is very important to note that this forecast is not finished. Indeed, it is never finished. Our goals change, just as life changes, and they need to be revisited.

In the following sections we will look at other components for financial wellbeing. It is possible, likely even, that going through these sections will lead to you rethink or challenge your assumptions. Be ready to go back to the beginning and make changes to your financial plan once you have finished the book. Continually refine your forecast so that it keeps up with your changing objectives.

PART THREE

CONTROL OVER FINANCES – MANAGING TODAY

In Part Two you spent some time looking at your income and expenses in order to project your financial future. Although this can be a pretty sobering exercise, it also allows clarity over what needs to be done to achieve your desired future. A lack of clarity and focus is one of the biggest causers of stress, and therefore one of the biggest enemies of wellbeing. So even if you don't like what you see, just the fact that you have a better understanding of the issues will reduce your stress levels.

In this section we will tackle another contributory factor to financial wellbeing: control of daily finances.

CONTROL

The important word here is *control*. Wellbeing does not necessarily come from spending more or less than you currently spend. Wellbeing arrives as a result of having *control* over what you spend.

THE IMPORTANCE OF CONTROL FOR WELLBEING

According to the Penny Brohn Cancer Centre, people diagnosed with cancer often feel frustrated by their lack of control over their illness. A common question that they ask is, "Is there anything that I can do?" A lot of the work of the centre is about providing an answer.

One of the drivers behind that question is the feeling of being out of control that the diagnosis of a life threatening illness brings. This lack of control significantly reduces feelings of wellbeing.

THE ONE ABOUT DRIVING TO WORK IN CENTRAL LONDON

I used to work in an office just off Oxford Circus in central London. Now, London undoubtedly has one of the most comprehensive public transport systems in the world. To get to work on public transport, one of my colleagues, George, would have had to take a train from his home in Surrey, then a bus or tube to the office.

Instead, George chose to drive to work. Every morning he would leave the house very early and sit in rush-hour traffic, crawling through London to get to the office. He would then pay a fortune in parking charges, work late to avoid the worst of the evening rush hour, then do it all again the next day. I once asked George why he didn't just take the trains like everyone else. "I like to be in control of my journey," was his reply. "If a train gets cancelled, I have to wait for another one, whereas in my car I am the one who decides which way to go."

I pointed out that this usually meant sitting with the engine off in queues of traffic each evening, but he was adamant that, for him, feeling in control was more important.

Some of us like to be in control more than others. What we are trying to avoid is the feeling of being *out of control*.

TIP: To achieve financial wellbeing, the first step is to understand your current spending, and then consider how your spending can be used to maximise wellbeing.

UNDERSTAND THE PRESENT

In Part One we spent a lot of time trying to work out what the future might look like. Then in Part Two we got a better understanding of the present and how it might affect the future. Simply knowing what you are spending each month should already be helping you feel in control. Now we want to work out how much you need to live on (subsistence income) and how much is left over (disposable income).

SUBSISTENCE INCOME

In Part Two you will have made a note of your current spending habits. Let's go back to those figures. How much of those expenditure are an absolute necessity? We're talking food and drink, housing, and clothing. We are also talking haircuts and holidays. But we're probably not talking the latest flat-screen TV, olives or another silk scarf. This is your subsistence income, an amount below which you simply could not countenance. Be true to yourself here – subsistence doesn't mean you have to cut out all happiness, and equally it doesn't mean that you have to buy a motorbike or spend £150 on a tablecloth.

DISPOSABLE INCOME

Now you should have an idea of how much of your income is spent on necessities and how much of it is left over. The extra amount left over is called your disposable income. This is the bit we are interested in, because this is the part of your income that can significantly impact your wellbeing.

Remember our underlying principle here is "know thyself". The more you understand and learn what makes you happy, the more you will be able to do those things and less of the things that do not. If you completed the income summary on page 27, you should now have your disposable income set out into categories. Now, consider each category of spending in turn and ask yourself this question: Does this expenditure make me happy? Let's look at some principles that might help you answer this question.

HOW TO SPEND YOUR MONEY TO ENHANCE WELLBEING

In deciding how to spend your money in order to generate wellbeing, it is worth looking at the longer-term impact of your spending.

SPENDING ON OTHERS

A study in Canada[6] found that certain spending can bring about happiness that disappears relatively quickly, whereas other spending – generally what they call "prosocial", i.e. spending on others –brings about longer-term wellbeing.

Researchers[7] in America gave a group of individuals either $5 or $20 and gave varying instructions on how to spend it, either on themselves or giving it to other people. The level of happiness reported at the end of the day was entirely dependent on how they spent the money and bore no relation to the actual amount of money they spent. We'll look at philanthropy in more detail in a moment.

It is possible to buy long-term wellbeing – but mainly when we spend on or with others.

Typical expenditure that is likely to increase wellbeing include:

- Gifts to charity
- Gifts to friends
- Experiences and memories
- Something that gets long-term use
- A dream item.

TIP: When reviewing expenditure, write down all major purchases over the last 12 months, perhaps anything costing over £100. Is that item still enhancing your wellbeing?

PROTECTION

Those monthly standing orders can quickly stack up, so it is important to have a good handle on where you are spending your money. Look through the "monthly bills" section of your summary of current expenditure. Are you using that National Trust membership? If not, either cancel it or, even better, *do* use it. Insurances and protection (life assurance, income protection, medical insurance, house and contents insurance) are vital for wellbeing. They provide a feeling of control because it means we know we are protected in the event of a catastrophic event – more on this later.

Of course, not everyone derives wellbeing from spending money on insurance policies.

THE ONE ABOUT THE IMMORTAL CLIENT

Many years ago I went to see a husband and wife. Their kids were grown but not yet financially stable. Among other areas, they were interested in life assurance so that if anything happened to them the kids would have their mortgages paid off. I wrote to them with some figures so that they could have an idea of costs. At our next meeting we came to the point on the agenda to discuss their life assurance needs.

"Thanks for the figures," said Mike. "But we're not going to go ahead."

"No problem. But can I ask why?" I was a little surprised.

"Of course, we've just decided it would be a waste of money to take out life assurance."

"Why's that, Mike?" I asked.

"Well, I'm not going to die. So there's no point."

More about protection on page 67.

RETAIL THERAPY

We live in a world drowning in marketing and advertising. Public spaces are crowded with billboards and adverts all seeking our attention. A typical approach to advertising is to create a desire. They instil a feeling of missing out if you do not have their product, or that a simple purchase will make you feel better or even make you a better person. This is no coincidence. One study[8] showed one group of people a sad film and another group a nature documentary. They then asked how much the participants would like to pay for a water bottle. The sad group offered four times more. It seems that being sad does encourage spending. We've even given it a name – retail therapy.

Retail therapy *does* increase wellbeing and it alleviates sadness – but how long term are the effects? Research suggests[9] that the wellbeing from buying physical goods wears off as we get used to them. We then go out and buy more goods to top up the wellbeing. If this spending increases debt and takes us further away from long-term objectives, then retail therapy could actually reduce wellbeing. Long-term impulse shopping – and the advertising that promotes it – can actually have a negative effect on your wellbeing.

TIP: If you see something you feel you really want, perhaps something that's a little over budget, wait two weeks. If you still want the item after two weeks (and can afford it), buy it. This is a great tip to apply to children asking for items.

"RE-TREASURING"

There are excellent books that explain the wellbeing to be gained from decluttering, going through our possessions and assessing what we really need to keep and what can be sold or thrown away. If we combine these two concepts – retail therapy and decluttering – we can come to a new conclusion. Perhaps we should hold on to something for only as long as it gives us feelings of wellbeing. At the stage when the treasured item crosses over to being paraphernalia and then clutter, we should get rid of it and enjoy the retail therapy of buying something else! This is a process we can think of as "re-treasuring."

BUY EXPERIENCES

Purchasing physical items creates wellbeing, which is temporary. Spending on others gives a more long-term increased wellbeing and the same has been found when spending money on experiences, such as travel. Purchasing experiences creates memories and the wellbeing from such experiences will last as long as the memories. Spending on experiences with others is therefore a double whammy!

We have spoken to many clients over the years about what they would do if they had more time on their hands and money was no object. The answers are invariably modest – few people seem to want to own a yacht, for example, even though this is perhaps the clichéd response. Instead, the most common response by far is travel. An extra holiday a year, taking a city break, a visit to family overseas – these deliver real long-term benefits to wellbeing.

TIP: Write down your memories. Ever since my children were born I have been keeping a journal of their childhoods. Everyday incidents and comments, things that make me and my wife laugh, things that happen to them that I think they'd like to be reminded of, and formative events. Occasionally I go back over old entries as I write new ones. I get huge satisfaction not only from the memories, but also from knowing that they are preserved for my children to enjoy one day too. I plan to make that journal into a book one day and will make only three copies – one for each of them, and one for me and my wife to enjoy.

SAVINGS AND INVESTMENTS

There is wellbeing to be had simply by getting closer to our dreams. Setting aside a modest monthly amount builds up and, after a few years, you find yourself closer to the objectives you set in Part One. Knowing, for example, that you might be able to retire a year or two earlier is likely to give far greater and longer-lasting wellbeing than purchasing a luxury item.

Mr and Mrs Procter were certainly happy to make some sacrifices in their current expenditure once they had seen in plain figures that it would enable them to retire three years earlier.

> **TIP:** Work out a figure that's approximately 20% of your disposable income per month, or an affordable figure that you know you could commit to. Pay that amount monthly by a standing order into a savings plan (perhaps ISA or pension). Rather like the goldfish that only grows to a size relative to the bowl it is kept in, your spending will contract to the amount you have available with minimal effect on your wellbeing.

REPAYING DEBT

Debt is an emotional issue. It may well be that a low interest rate or a good fixed deal would suggest keeping a mortgage is a good idea. High-risk individuals might even choose to refinance in order to make an exciting investment. In general, however, we humans do not like having debt. The wellbeing from living in an unencumbered property will often be greater than the wellbeing from getting a slightly better return by investing elsewhere. Interestingly, surveys[10] have shown that we tend to pay off small debts first, even when the larger debt carries a higher interest rate.

TIP: Your aim should be to reduce your debt as quickly as possible, starting with the more expensive debt. If you have multiple debts, write down the details next to each: amount of debt, term to repayment (if applicable), monthly repayment amount, and most importantly, the interest rate. Focus your repayment on the debt with the highest interest rates.

PHILANTHROPY

As we have seen, helping others can be a significant source of wellbeing. Whether this comes from helping a friend in need, offering some of your time to a sports club or charity, or making financial donations, we all have our own attitude to charity. Philanthropy can range from buying a sandwich for a homeless person to making a bequest in your will to setting up your own charitable trust. In order to maximise the wellbeing from your giving, it is worth taking a few moments to consider your approach to philanthropy.

Here are a few factors you may wish to take into account[11]:

- Greater wellbeing comes from planned, rather than reactive, giving. This is because planned giving can be a joyous feeling of helping others, whereas reactive giving is often fuelled by feelings of guilt
- Donors most often give in an ad-hoc way, but prefer committed giving via direct debit
- Three in five donors pay close or extremely close attention to how their donation will be used. A personal connection is also often very influential. It seems wellbeing can be derived from seeing the effect of the donation
- The very fact of giving creates wellbeing, independent of the

worthiness of the cause. Removing feelings of dependence on a sum of money can be liberating

- As wealth accumulates, there often comes a time when individuals have a moment of revelation when they realise their true relationship with money. This can result in a change in priorities and an increase in philanthropy
- Giving is not just for the wealthy. Wellbeing can be derived from donations that involve sacrifice just as much, possibly more, as donations from surplus.

A key part of wellbeing is having a sense of purpose in life. Philanthropy can be food for the soul, whether it's the giving of money or the giving of time. For some individuals, this act can create a sense of having found the thing they are destined to do.

CONCLUSION

You should now have a better idea of your current spending, and how that spending can be used to maximise wellbeing.

You should be able to make changes so that you focus your spending on the areas that will increase your wellbeing. You might also increase how much you are setting aside into savings and pensions in order to achieve those long-term aims.

PART **FOUR**

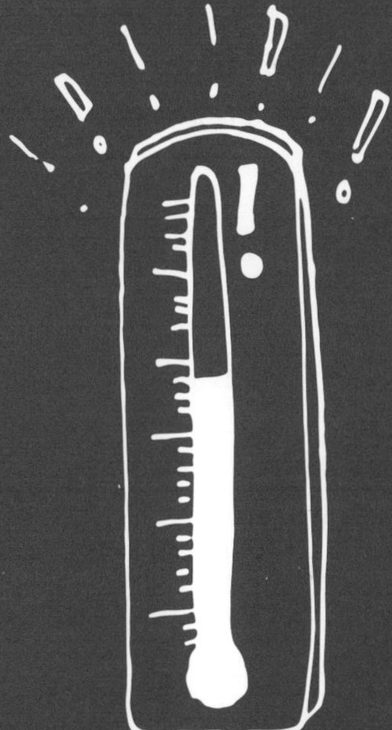

FINANCIAL SHOCKS

So far, we have shown that by clarifying what we want from the future and creating a path to get there, we increase our wellbeing. We also focused on today and what changes we could make to increase wellbeing and, perhaps, bring the future forward a little. Maybe this even brought a few dreams a little closer to reality.

Now for the third part of our plan: let's go back to looking toward the future and determine how we can increase our ability to cope with a financial shock.

INCREASING THE ABILITY TO COPE

Our aim is to increase wellbeing—or avoid it being reduced. We can achieve this in relation to financial shocks by:

- Avoiding them
- Preparing for them
- Understanding them.

By definition, a financial shock is something that is beyond our control. As such, it is not just the shock itself, but also the worry that the shock might happen, that must be addressed.

WHAT COULD POSSIBLY GO WRONG?

Financial shocks that could directly impact our wellbeing include:

- Death
- Illness
- Investment losses
- Redundancy
- Debt/bankruptcy
- Changes in legislation (e.g., taxes).

The extent to which our worries about the future affect our wellbeing is different for everyone. In keeping with the principle in this book of "know thyself," it is important for you to think about what might go wrong and how you would possibly handle it.

This can be uncomfortable territory. It is not uncommon for people to avoid making a will because they do not like to think about their own mortality. Knowing that you are prepared for a financial shock, however, is more likely to improve your wellbeing.

So take the time to think about what might go wrong, put in place measures to reduce the impact of those shocks, and feel better knowing you won't have to think about them again for some time!

SOME BASIC FINANCIAL PLANNING PRINCIPLES

When constructing a financial plan, there are a few simple principles to follow. Increased wellbeing can be derived from the future looking a little less uncertain.

EMERGENCY FUNDS

A 2014 survey by Barclays[12] showed that there is greater wellbeing gained from having a sum of money set aside than there is from having a pay rise.

Whether you are embarking on your life of wealth creation or deciding how to make the assets you have already built up last throughout your later years, the first plank of a financial plan is to establish an emergency fund. The characteristic of these funds are typically:

- Cash (no investment risk)
- Not concerned about returns
- Instantly accessible

- An amount approximately equal to six months of expenditure
- Not to be used except in a real emergency.

The six-month figure is one we use as a guide for the minimum amount of funds you'd need to support yourself if you were, for example, to contract a serious illness or lose your job. You may choose to have more than six months' expenditure if that makes you feel better – and increases your wellbeing.

TIP: Online banking often allows you to nickname your different bank accounts. Set up a new account and call it "Safety Net." Transfer in an amount equal to at least six months' expenditure – or set up a regular payment to build up to this figure.

Every time you check your balance online you should be able to see this account and take comfort from the fact that you have funds set aside for emergencies.

Knowing that you have sufficient funds set aside that will cover your bills and expenses for six months in the event of any future financial shock will enhance your wellbeing.

Simply having a plan to tackle a financial shock that may come your way will help to reduce stress.

A LITTLE AND OFTEN

For those starting out on wealth creation, the discipline of setting up a monthly payment can be key. A modest sum automatically leaving your account – that you'll forget about – may turn into the bedrock of your investment portfolio a few years down the line. By all means add lump sums when spare cash becomes available, but don't overcommit, as this might negatively affect your quality of life now.

Fear of the unknown is the arch enemy of wellbeing. Reduce the unknown by doing something about it today, no matter how small. This is a lesson we can pass on to our children.

START EARLY

Any young person will tell you that the last thing you want to do when you finally have a bit of disposable income in your pocket is put it away somewhere for the future. Any older person will tell you that the earlier you start saving, the easier things are later in life.

"Look after the pennies and the pounds look after themselves" is a good habit to adopt at a young age.

THE ONE ABOUT THE TRIPS TO LONDON

My father had a large jar in his bedroom. Every night as he undressed for bed he would take whatever coins were in his pocket and throw them into the jar. When the jar was full, once a year or so, we would take a family trip to London for the day. We loved this trip to London; I still have a clear memory of feeding pigeons in Hyde Park. My brother and I would excitedly empty the coins all over the lounge carpet and separate the different denominations into piles before putting them into bank bags.

What none of us knew was that Mum was doing the same thing with pound notes from Dad's wallet, which would help replace the car every few years!

PROTECTION

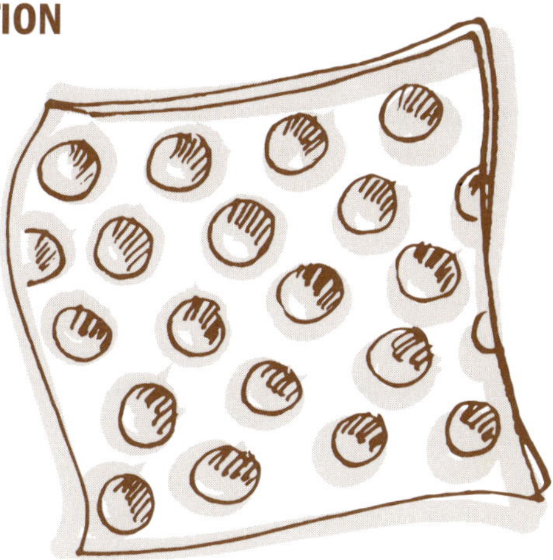

There are many risks we face in life, some more likely to happen than others. Almost all of these risks can be covered by some sort of insurance policy, from being abducted by aliens to immaculate conception. Let's look at the most common risks and what might be an appropriate level of protection for you.

PROTECTION – DEATH

Your life assurance needs depend on whether anyone is financially dependent upon you. A single person may have no need for life assurance. However, anyone with children should consider life assurance virtually compulsory.

There are typically three needs that life assurance fulfils:

1. Repayment of debt
2. Short-term needs
3. Ongoing living expenses.

The policy should take into account other assets. For example, someone with a £100,000 mortgage and £100,000 in a pension fund might not need additional assurance to repay debt. In a case like this, the pension could be earmarked to pay off the mortgage on death, although other types of coverage may still be needed.

A couple in their mid-thirties, with two children aged four and six, each earning £25,000 per annum and a mortgage of £150,000 should therefore have three different policies as a minimum (assuming there are no other assets):

1. £150,000 lump-sum payable on the death of either one of the couple so that the surviving spouse no longer has mortgage repayments to meet. End date should match the mortgage. The £150,000 payable can reduce over the period (if repaying mortgage) or stay the same (if paying the interest on the mortgage only). Both types of policy are available.
2. A lump sum (perhaps £50,000) payable when the first of the couple dies so that the surviving spouse doesn't have to think about money for a while.
3. An income of £25,000 per annum, payable when the first of the couple dies, to end when the second child is no longer financially dependent (e.g. two years after education is completed).

Some people just like to see cash in their bank account to feel better, and that is fine – as long as the objectives identified in Part One and mapped out in Part Two are achievable.

LOSS OF INCOME THROUGH ILLNESS

There are two main ways to protect yourself in the event of a serious illness. Critical Illness coverage pays a lump sum when one of a range of specific illnesses is diagnosed, whereas Income Protection (also known as Permanent Health Insurance or PHI for short) pays a monthly amount in the event of any illness that results in not being able to work for more than a set period of time.

Both types can be rather expensive, especially later in life. Of course, this is because the chance of using the coverage is that much greater – which, one could argue, makes the coverage all the more necessary.

MEDICAL INSURANCE

It is also common to take out insurance for the cost of medical treatment. In the UK this tends to be for getting treatment quickly or for areas not otherwise covered, such as dentistry. Whether you will increase your wellbeing as a result of taking out such coverage depends entirely on how worried you are about the issue.

PRIORITISING PROTECTION

There are many other types of protection available. Assuming you are on a limited budget, how do you decide which coverage is most important to you?

In our experience, ensuring your dependents are going to be looked after in the event of death is the one essential area of protection. In keeping with our "know thyself" theme, take some time with your loved ones discussing other eventualities and how you can insure yourself against them.

TIP: List the areas that concern you, then place them in a grid like this (these are just some suggestions):

	DEATH	SERIOUS ILLNESS	VET COSTS	BURGLARY	DAMAGE TO MUSICAL INSTRUMENT
DEATH					
SERIOUS ILLNESS					
VET COSTS					
BURGLARY					
DAMAGE TO MUSICAL INSTRUMENT					

Next, consider which you are most concerned about by pitting each of the areas of concern against the other. For example, which would be the higher priority, buying life assurance or pet insurance?

You should end up with a chart that looks something like this:

	DEATH	SERIOUS ILLNESS	VET COSTS	BURGLARY	DAMAGE TO MUSICAL INSTRUMENT
DEATH	X	X	X	X	X
SERIOUS ILLNESS	DEATH	X	X	X	X
VET COSTS	DEATH	VET COSTS	X	X	X
BURGLARY	DEATH	SERIOUS ILLNESS	VET COSTS	X	X
DAMAGE TO MUSICAL INSTRUMENT	DEATH	SERIOUS ILLNESS	VET COSTS	DAMAGE TO MUSICAL INSTRUMENT	X

The frequency of each area of concern within the grid will provide your order of priority for how to spend your budget on insuring your risks. Note: this system can be used whenever you need to prioritise a list of conflicting objectives.

BUSINESS PROTECTION

If you are owner or part-owner of a small business, you may well see your business as your pension. Like any asset, the business should be protected against risk.

Almost every business has fire insurance and a disaster recovery plan for getting the business back and working again quickly. But how many have a plan in case a key employee or director dies or contracts a life-threatening illness?

THE ONE ABOUT THE DIRECTORS WHO WERE BEST FRIENDS

Mike and Zaheer were best friends and equal owners of a small business. Zaheer was married to Linda, with two young children. We recommended the two directors take out shareholder protection. This meant that if anything happened to either of them, the surviving director would have the funds to buy the shares from the widow. Zaheer never got around to completing the paperwork. Linda nagged him, but he was only 35 and treated it all as a bit of a joke.

One morning Zaheer woke up and suffered a fatal heart attack. It was completely out of the blue and everyone was shocked. At the funeral, Mike gave a wonderful eulogy.

A few months later, when she was able to start looking at such things, Linda decided she wasn't interested in the business and offered to sell the shares to Mike. Mike did not react as Linda had expected. He refused to pay anything for the shares and threatened to shut the company down if Linda didn't give him the shares for nothing. Several years of legal arguments ensued, which resulted in Linda receiving a payment for only a fraction of the real value of the shares.

If Zaheer had filled in those forms and set up life assurance, not only would the shares have been protected, but Linda would not have had the stress of the legal battle with Mike.

CONCLUSION

Reducing the potential impact of a financial shock will help increase wellbeing and reduce stress. However, the extent of the wellbeing gained will vary among different people. Some people like to have everything planned and ordered; others are willing to accept a bit of risk and hate wasting money on the unknown. Knowing yourself and getting the balance of your insurances right is an important step for financial wellbeing.

INVESTMENT LOSSES – RISK TOLERANCE

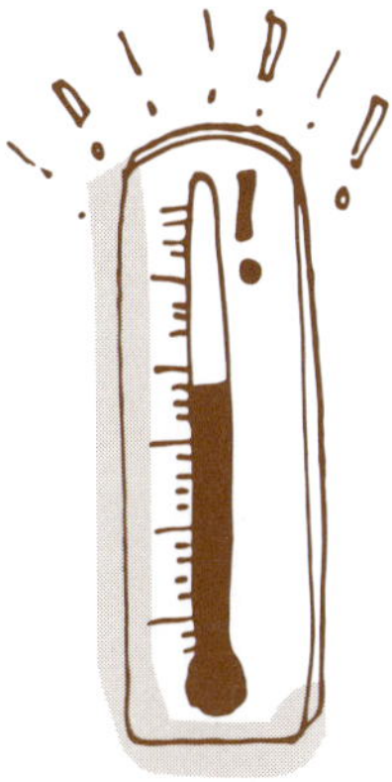

This section will help you understand your attitude toward investment risk and how to align it with your financial plan.

One definition of investing could be: "The act of placing money in a place where the returns are completely out of your control." This isn't a traditional definition, but it does rather sum up how investing can feel!

Risk tolerance – how much investment risk you're comfortable with – is a detailed and often fascinating subject. Understanding yourself and how you react to various levels of risk may take a little time, but it is absolutely key to long-term wellbeing.

RISK QUESTIONNAIRES

Questionnaires are available to help assess your risk tolerance. You can go online yourself and try one. Finametrica has been studying the nature of risk for many years, and its comprehensive questionnaire is available at www.myrisktolerance.com. There are plenty of other simpler, free tools online.

It is worth bearing in mind that that by gauging your risk tolerance through a questionnaire, you will not arrive at the end of the assessment process. Risk tolerance itself is a personality trait, which can easily be determined. However, other features of a risk profile are both harder to assess and more likely to change over time – and are likely to drive action.

UNDERSTANDING YOUR OWN RISK TOLERANCE

A person who is averse to investment risk may find holding volatile investments such as shares to be stressful. Therefore, this type of investment will have a negative effect on the wellbeing of such a person. Conversely, someone happy to accept short-term fluctuations in order to achieve long-term goals may find it stressful to hold all of his or her assets in cash.

When we first ask clients to assess their attitude to risk, they generally have little idea how to answer, especially if they have no previous investing experience. On a scale of one to five, where five is the highest and one lowest, most people asked about risk for the first time tend to rate themselves as a three, right in the middle. What they are really doing is not making a decision. And this is because they don't understand the question; they need more information.

THE ONE ABOUT EVERYONE ELSE'S RISK

Perhaps the best example of how *not* to rate your attitude to investment risk was given by one client during our initial meeting. We had asked him to assess his own level of risk, as a way of starting a conversation on the subject. He thought about the question for a while, then asked, "Do you know, I'm not really sure. What does everyone else do?"

An individual's risk profile is highly personal and depends on a host of different factors in addition to risk tolerance. This includes:

- Experience
- Necessity
- Capacity for financial loss
- Timescale
- Income Requirements
- Financial position and earning capacity
- Age
- Emotion.

Let's look at each in turn to understand your risk profile better.

TIP: When reading these next sections, make a note of your emotional reaction to the points being made, which will help you start to build a picture of your risk tolerance.

EXPERIENCE

Having previous investing experience may help a person make better decisions, but surveys have shown that a person's actual level of risk tolerance does not tend to change with time. It would seem that our emotional response to investment risk is programmed into us. Many investors never learn about their risk tolerance, making the same mistakes time after time and reducing their wellbeing.

THE ONE ABOUT NASDAQ AND THE MASSES

NASDAQ is a stock market in USA and Canada. In the early 2000s it was the epicentre of the dot-com boom and was posting eye-watering gains. In the month just before the market peaked, it recorded its highest ever inflow of new money. In the month that later turned out to be the peak, this record was broken as even more investors put their money into the dot-com sector. Just after the peak, the index plummeted. In that month a new record was set for investors leaving the market.

Logic tells us to "buy low, sell high", but in practice investors often do exactly the opposite, entering a market at the top and selling at the bottom.

If you have had many years of watching your investments go up and down over and over, you tend to take a more philosophical view of market fluctuations. Your behaviour changes, but your long-term level of risk tolerance does not.

We have met a number of people who declare themselves low-risk investors after one experience of investing. They often bought at the top of the market, saw their investments go down in value, then sold somewhere near the bottom of the market. By the same token, we have met people who set up their own investment portfolio during a rising market and think investing is easy and that they have it cracked.

It is important to be wary of experience, for it can be misleading when assessing your attitude to risk. Perceptions of risk will cloud our own judgment. Experience can be misleading. It is the mermaid of investment management: appealing and seductive, yet potentially calling you to your doom.

NECESSITY – HOW MUCH RISK DO YOU NEED TO TAKE?

The cash-flow model that you constructed in Part Two used an assumption for future growth. We talked a little in that section of the "chicken-and-egg" nature of how much risk you need to take in order to achieve your objectives, and setting objectives that are realistic to the potential growth.

Overestimating your growth assumptions leads to taking more risk than you are comfortable with. This in turn can lead to losses that you cannot afford. The level of growth you need to take should therefore be balanced by your capacity for loss.

CAPACITY FOR FINANCIAL LOSS

One definition of the capacity for financial loss is the amount of money a person is willing and able to lose and still live a decent life. This brings about a possible contradiction: how much people are willing to lose may well be different than what they are able to lose. This shows that there are actually two parts to assessing your capacity for financial loss:

- Physical capacity for loss – at what point is your lifestyle going to be affected (how much are you "able" to lose)
- Emotional capacity for loss – at what point would you take some form of action (how much are you "willing" to lose).

PHYSICAL CAPACITY FOR LOSS

The "ability" to lose money describes how much the value of your investments could fall before your current lifestyle is affected. And yet even this is complicated – no investment makes a loss until it is cashed in. The capital value may fluctuate, but lifestyle may not be affected unless the income levels change. This is a calculation that is difficult to skate over. Financial planners use complicated software that displays the impact that multiple possible events would have on a person's lifestyle.

For our purposes we need something simpler. First, ask yourself these three questions about your investments:

1. If your investments suffered a financial shock, do you have alternative sources of income to fall back on?

This might include the ability to earn an income, assets you could sell, or perhaps frozen pensions from previous jobs. It is also the thinking behind not investing everything you own and spreading a portfolio among a variety of different investment types (called asset classes), which spreads risk.

2. Do you understand the risks involved in the investment?
By how much could the investment, realistically, decrease in value? Sometimes investment products that seem the safest can carry the greatest potential losses. Be wary of the word "guaranteed" for anything other than bank accounts, for example. Will the income received from such an investment be affected if the capital goes down?

3. If the investment, and the income from it, went down by 30%, how would your lifestyle be affected?
The 30% figure is an arbitrary one; the investment you choose may be able to fluctuate more or less than this. However, it is a useful benchmark.

EMOTIONAL CAPACITY FOR LOSS

Many people mistake a change in risk *perception* as a change in risk *tolerance*. An individual's risk tolerance tends not to change over time. However, a person's perception of risk will more than likely change. Older investors close to or in retirement might worry more about investment volatility than those in their 30s who will not need to access their pension until they are in their 60s.

Really understanding your investments, and your reaction to how they change, is key to financial wellbeing. Taking the time to understand your physical capacity for loss may well have an effect on your emotional capacity for loss.

TIMESCALE

Risk may reduce over time. What may seem a disaster one day may barely be a blip on the charts when viewed in the context of 20 years.

THE ONE ABOUT THE 1987 STOCK MARKET CRASH

Throughout the first ten months of 1987, the UK stock market went rapidly upward. Then, in October 1987, the market crashed, on a day to be known henceforth as "Black Monday". Not only were the gains of the year wiped out, but the market continued to plummet downward, as if the losses would never end. For the last few months of that year, markets slowly recovered from the seemingly disastrous lows of that terrible day in October.

Meanwhile, Fred and Vera travelled the whole year. Fred checked his investments on January 1 and didn't look at them again until they returned from their travels on the last day of December.

"How did the investments do while we were away?" Vera asked.

"They went up by about 4%, and we received 4% in dividends," Fred replied. "Must have been a quiet year for the stock market."

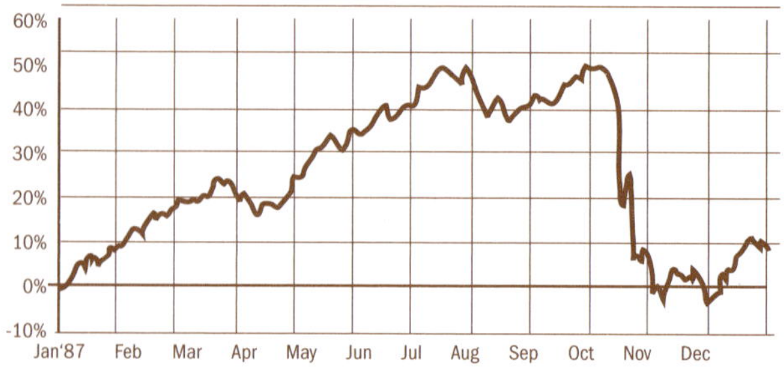

Any risk-based investment portfolio should have a minimum time period of at least three years, preferably five, to allow for the ups and downs to smooth out. Some investment portfolios are never cashed out, but are handed down for generations. In such cases, changes in the value of the portfolio might be less of a concern than changes in the income it produces. Therefore, the anticipated timescale of the investment should be taken into account when assessing the level of risk to be taken.

TIP: Long-term investment should not feel like gambling. If you do want that feeling, gamble with a small part of your overall wealth only and have a strategy for the rest that is aligned to your financial plan.

INCOME REQUIREMENT

Risk to capital can be higher than the risk to income. The value of a property (capital), for example, is largely irrelevant as long as the tenant continues to pay the rent (income). Consequently, the level of risk can be targeted on capital if the main focus of the investment is to provide income, perhaps by investing in an asset that provides a steady income.

Investment risk and understanding what you enjoy in life are heavily linked. Financial wellbeing may vary depending on the degree of income received from an investment. Your wellbeing may be better served by a reduction in your income – which requires a better understanding of lifestyle and general expenditure – than from taking a level of investment risk with which you are uncomfortable.

FINANCIAL POSITION AND EARNING CAPACITY

It may seem logical that people with other assets or a significant surplus income can take a higher amount of risk with their investment portfolio, safe in the knowledge that if the funds were to go down in value, they could be replaced. This is not always the case, however; our risk tolerance is relatively fixed and not necessarily affected by external factors such as wealth.

THE ONE ABOUT WALLY'S RETIREMENT INCOME

Wally ran his own business for many years. He knew how much money he wanted to live on and had undertaken comprehensive financial planning. One day, when Wally was in his 60s, we calculated that a combination of interest rates at the time and the value of his pension meant that he could cash everything in and obtain the income he wanted for him and his wife.

Wally stopped work a few weeks later. He sold all his investments in his pension and bought an annuity (Gave his pension fund to an insurance company in exchange for a guaranteed income for life). Wally knew it wasn't the most tax-efficient use of the money and his children, while being looked after, would not benefit from a sizeable pension fund. But purchasing the annuity was right for Wally because it gave him the one thing he craved – certainty of income in his retirement.

AGE

Being old does not automatically reduce risk. Age may either be highly relevant or completely irrelevant to the level of investment risk an investor is willing to take. We have clients in their 90s who want to keep investments in a risk-based portfolio. Sometimes this is because it gives them something to do or perhaps because they want to maximise the amount of money they leave behind. We also have clients in their 20s who wish to take minimal investment risk because they don't like the idea of their modest portfolio being subject to volatility. In other words, your age is not a significant determining factor in your attitude to investment risk.

EMOTION

Sometimes we are irrational. We act on emotion.

Many people choose to repay their mortgage when rates are lower than they might get from an investment because they want to be free of debt. As long as your actions are consistent with your motivations and objectives, then emotion-driven decisions are right for you. With one caveat: be very wary of the "gut feeling" that involves investing more than you can really afford.

BEHAVIOURAL INVESTING (AKA, DON'T PANIC)

There are some who advocate making all investment decisions based on what everyone else is doing instead of analysing the markets or companies they want to invest in. This approach is known as "behavioural investing".

The investment management company, Vanguard Asset Management[13], attempts to put figures on the benefits their financial advisers make to their clients' investment decisions. They estimate that behavioural coaching alone can add between 1% and 2% to the performance of investments each year.

The media has a habit of focusing on bad news. The phrase, "Today billions of pounds were wiped off the value of shares" is rarely followed a week later by, "Billions of pounds have been added back onto the value of shares". As a consequence, we, the general public, make investment decisions with our hearts rather than our heads.

TIP: One way of approaching investments is to do what everyone isn't. Although this should not be taken too literally (a share may be cheap for a good reason), it is not a bad principle to keep in the back of your mind when assessing investment markets.

CONCLUSION

Wellbeing can come from taking practical steps to reduce the impact of financial shocks. The amount of action we can take will often be determined by our disposable income. How much we want to spend on life assurance, for example, versus how much we want to spend on our holidays, is a difficult trade off. Therefore, we must understand ourselves better to determine how to structure our finances and investments; this is key to increasing our financial wellbeing.

PART FIVE

THE LUXURY OF CHOICE

We have now set up a financial plan aligned with our objectives, and we have made a few changes to how we manage our money. The next step is to address the ability to have options in life. By following the processes and reaching this part of the book, you will have already considered some of your options. But, are there more options that you haven't yet noticed or considered?

The first half of this section will examine how to increase and recognise your options. The second part will challenge some of the standard thinking about financial planning and wealth in order to seek greater appreciation of what we have, and thereby generate wellbeing without the need for wealth.

OPTIONS FROM WEALTH

Wellbeing comes from having your requirements for life and your finances well matched. I might quite like to own a chateau in France with my own team of servants and a recording studio in the basement, but the acceptance that this is not going to happen will give me more wellbeing than clinging to a hope that it might. On the other hand, if I recognise that what I really want from this dream is the ability to record my own music, then perhaps a modest investment in recording software for my home computer might give me a considerable boost in wellbeing.

TIP: One word that we might associate with people who have strong financial wellbeing is "satisfied". Their quality of life and standard of living are in line with their requirements.

There are two ways of achieving this equilibrium:

1. Increase your standard of living to match your life requirements
2. Bring your life requirements in line with your standard of living.

Wealth does bring options: choice of holiday, what work to do, whether to work at all or to retire, are all choices that come with accumulating wealth.

To achieve the desired financial wellbeing, the options available need to be the right ones *for us*. Of course, many options are not linked to money at all. We therefore need to look at all the **options money can provide** and how to generate the **right ones for us as individuals.**

SELF-LIMITING BELIEFS

Are we stopping ourselves from seeing all the options available to us? Our view of the world is made up of the collection of our experiences and our reactions to them. This creates a belief system that inevitably informs our choices and options. These very beliefs, however, may be limiting our options.

Here are a few examples of self-limiting beliefs:

- I can't do X because of Y
- I won't be happy until I have enough money
- I don't have enough resources (a tactic to give ourselves permission to remain stuck)
- I have too many responsibilities to have fun
- Earning money is hard work
- I'm expected to ... (by whom?)
- It's just the way things are (collective assumption)
- Options only increase with wealth.

The key point to remember is that beliefs are not truths.

Beliefs are the result of our world view, created by a lifetime of experiences. It is easy to allow our beliefs to define us. They shape our thinking and our actions, prevent us from seeing opportunities, and can discourage us from even trying at all. It is difficult to change one's beliefs and fixed ideas. There is frequently a time lag between changes in our thinking and actual changes in our emotional state. Even when we recognise that something isn't logical or rational, there will be an internal forceful debate between our rational and irrational thoughts over a period of time. Assistance from a third party, such as a qualified coach, can be useful in identifying and challenging our beliefs.

TIP: Here is one approach to break the pattern of self-limiting beliefs:

1. Identify the thought patterns, fixed ideas, and beliefs
2. Test assumptions and challenges: How do you know this is

correct? (It can of course be a perfectly logical and rational truth)

3. Acknowledge that this is a belief and not the truth
4. Replace with new, more effective belief (e.g., replace "either/or" with "both/and")
5. Act as if your new belief is true.

As we have said before, it is not really possible to challenge yourself, so this is an exercise best undertaken with someone who knows you well or, even better, someone experienced in such techniques, such as a coach.

THE ONE ABOUT THE CLIENT WHO WAS RELUCTANT TO MEET

Grace was 56 and had been a client and friend for many years. She worked for a company she didn't like and was stressed. She and her partner kept their finances separate. Over the years, Grace had bought a few properties, as well as used our services to build up a pension fund. There were a few outstanding mortgages to repay and Grace was focusing her income on debt reduction. She was always the sort of person to say "yes" to any requests for help – and was consequently always busy.

With her kids leaving home and trying to make their way in the world, she had her head down, just getting through life. Over the years, we had tried to talk to her about ideal levels of income, what she wanted her life to look like, and doing things for herself rather than for others. We asked Grace to come in for a meeting, with her partner. She procrastinated and it took six months to find a date that worked. On the scheduled day her partner arrived but she called to cancel, saying she was stuck in a meeting. We said we weren't going anywhere until she arrived. When the meeting got underway, we presented her with an analysis of her financial position. We concluded that if she sold two properties, used the proceeds to repay some debt and drew on some of her pension fund, she would have enough to retire.

We delivered the punchline. "Grace, you are now working because you want to, not because you have to." After a few tears, we all discussed what Grace might do next. Three weeks later she resigned and became a self employed consultant. Within two months she was working just as hard, but not on Fridays, and only with clients of her choosing.

GENERATING MORE OPTIONS

If you have recognised some of your self-limiting beliefs and perhaps challenged them, you may be ready to create more options for yourself. The process of generating more options is really about being creative, using lateral thinking to break out from the limitations of your current world view. For example, it is typically the case that the first answer we have to a question will be based on existing thinking.

TIP: When trying to come up with new solutions, write down all your ideas as fast as possible, then set that list aside and start again.

Here are a few suggestions to help you discover more options:

- Talk with someone, preferably a professional, such as a financial planner or a coach. It is very difficult to challenge your own thinking
- Questions should be open to explore more ideas: "What else ... ?"
- Use brainstorming – the process of creating ideas without limitations and without judging them
- Get all the ideas out before considering their merits
- Use questions that suspend limiting thinking: "If there were no limits on ... what would you do then?"
- Use questions that break the rules: "What if you didn't need to ... ?"

You are aiming to list as many options as possible, with as little evaluation and judgment as possible. Once the list is complete, you can then evaluate them for suitability, feasibility, and how well they will achieve the objectives and motivations that you identified in Part One. If you dismiss an idea, go back and test whether it was dismissed because it contradicts one of your self-limiting beliefs.

TIP: If you are trying to solve a problem, write down as many possible solutions as you can think of (you will find it easier to discuss this with another person). The key is not to think about the merits of each idea, but just get all the ideas down that you can. If you haven't thought of something really dumb, you haven't gone on for long enough. Only when you are convinced that all ideas are out should you then go back and evaluate them.

THE ONE ABOUT THE IMPORTANCE OF GENERATING MORE OPTIONS WHILE YOU CAN

Alison had been running her own small business for 20 years. Divorced with a ten-year-old son, she was not happy in her work, but could not see any alternative. Like many small business owners, with staff and clients to look after, she felt trapped.

One day Alison was jogging, listening to music through her earphones. After looking both ways she crossed a road. A car she had not noticed hit her. She landed on the bonnet, breaking her neck, and then fell onto the road. Alison was conscious and will never forget the lorry driver who held her hand while they waited for the ambulance to arrive. A police officer spoke to her in the hospital, and she asked him whether her son had been told. The man wasn't sure how to answer. He explained that he was the officer who gets called to the hospital when someone has died. He wasn't expecting her to be alive.

Two years later Alison and I had lunch. She was nearing the completion of a careful winding down of her business and was planning to live abroad for a year before deciding what to do next with her life. She spoke of lying on the road, very much aware of the seriousness of what had just happened. The very first thought that came into Alison's mind at that moment was, "I have to change my life."

CHALLENGING STANDARD THINKING ABOUT PERSONAL FINANCE

Some self-limiting beliefs are formed through assumptions. There are a number of accepted wisdoms in financial planning that limit options. Simply by looking at things a different way, perhaps we can increase our options and thereby our financial wellbeing.

WHY ARE WE SO OBSESSED WITH ACCUMULATING CAPITAL?

Let's go back to Part Two for a moment and look at those financial scenarios that people most commonly ask us to model: retirement or change of work; travel; leaving a legacy; repayment of mortgage; care-home fees.

They all have one thing in common: they all require income, not capital.

With the exception of mortgage repayment – which could come from increasing income to cover only the mortgage payments and not repaying the mortgage itself – who benefits if you die owning your own home?

We work for income. Hopefully we work for pleasure, too, although that is usually something of a luxury, especially early in life. Hopefully enjoying our work becomes an option again later in life as we build up our wealth and therefore options.

Slowly we accumulate wealth: investment portfolios, houses, pension funds. What do we want from these assets? Ultimately, unless it is owned for fun, an asset is only as useful as the income it can provide.

THE ONE ABOUT OWNING A FLAT IN LONDON

A new client came to see us. We discussed his hopes and dreams for the future, which centred on reducing his work hours because he enjoyed what he did, and travelling more, especially with his family. Among the questions we asked to encourage a little dreaming was, "What would you do if money was no object?" Like many of our clients, his response was relatively modest.

"I'd buy a flat in London. And I'd probably collect art," he said.

"And what would that give you?" we asked.

"Well," he replied, "my wife and I used to live in London and we do like going back there, so it would be lovely to be able to visit more often. And we've always appreciated art, so it would be nice to build up a collection."

We asked the client if he would mind if we challenged him on this, which he was comfortable with. "Would you not be able to visit London without owning a property there?" we asked. "Could you not enjoy art without owning it?"

We pointed out that by tying his capital up in owning things, he might actually reduce the experiences he could buy. By staying in hotels instead of owning a flat in London, they could go to other cities and visit art galleries around the world.

PENSIONS TIE UP YOUR MONEY

A pension fund provides income when we retire. We don't need access to the fund itself; rather, we need something to live on that will replace our salaries. This was the principle behind the huge company pension schemes (then known as "final salary" schemes; now known as "defined benefit"). The purpose of these schemes was to provide income in retirement. The underlying fund, which provided the income, was not passed down to the next of kin upon death. There usually would be an ongoing (albeit reduced) income for the surviving spouse; but after that, nothing. And then Robert Maxwell fell off his boat and everything changed. His plundering of the Mirror Group pension scheme was uncovered and new legislation was introduced to protect members of company pension funds. The long-term result of this was the closure of all such schemes, except for those in the public sector. But what has been lost in the process is the comfort of a fixed income in retirement that so many of the older generation currently enjoy.

The purpose of a pension is to lock away funds until retirement. It is advisable to use your pension to build up a fund that will provide a subsistence level of income in retirement. You can also use other assets to build up funds that you can cash in, if desired.

TIP: For some people – perhaps in ill health – having access to the capital in their pension may be a good thing. While for others, taking the whole pension as a lump sum, incurring a tax charge, and then reinvesting for income may not be a sensible move. Specialist advice should be obtained by anyone thinking of taking pension benefits in any form.

THE ONE ABOUT TAKING CASH FROM A PENSION TO BUY A FLAT

Recently a friend told me how delighted he was about the forthcoming "pension freedom" rules. He was planning to withdraw his pension fund of around £60,000 in one go and use the money to buy a flat, with the aid of a mortgage, which he would then rent out.

I asked for his reasoning behind this move. He said, "I hate pensions. I just want to get my hands on the money."

I pointed out that he would be paying a large amount of tax on the pension he was cashing in, more than if he would pay if he took it as income.

"Yes," he replied, "but I'll be able to get my hands on my money."

I then pointed out that he was buying an asset, a property, which might be difficult to sell if the property market was to flatten and he needed to sell quickly – he would pay tax on at least part of the income (as with the pension). He would pay tax on any growth of the property (unlike the pension). The property would now be inside his estate and potentially attract inheritance tax on his death (unlike the pension). And finally, I told him that the property would give him an income – just as the pension fund would have.

"Yes," he replied after a pause. "But I'll be able to get my hands on my money."

INVESTING FOR INCOME OR GROWTH?

When an income is required, it is common to seek investments through which regular payments will be received. This could be rent from a property, dividends from shares, interest on a loan, or maybe gilts (coupon). An alternative approach, however, could be to take income from cashing in the capital.

Suppose you buy some shares for £100 and they are paying a dividend of 5%. This means you get a regular income of £5 a year. Alternatively, you buy a share for £100 that is paying a 0% dividend, but the price of the shares rises to £105. You cash in the £5, which provides your "income".

One advantage of this route can be that you pay less tax. Cashing in the growth means you can use your capital gains tax allowance, so you might receive the payment tax-free. The income route may require income tax at your highest rate.

Obviously the income received from such investments depends on your circumstances (whether or not you have used your capital gains tax allowance elsewhere, for example). Often companies that distribute profits to shareholders through dividends tend to be less risky than companies that reinvest profit for growth and therefore pay low dividends. Nevertheless, it may be worth challenging the conventional wisdom that income should come from investments that pay income. In some cases it is worth considering partial encashment of capital as an alternative.

THE ABANDONMENT OF HOPE

Some would suggest that the secret to happiness is the abandonment of hope. Perhaps a more palatable word for the same principle is “acceptance”.

Children often dream of becoming famous or rich, being a pop star or representing their favourite sports team. I remember the realisation that I was never going to open the bowling for the England cricket team. It came as something of a relief.

Can you remember your age when you realised you were unlikely to fulfil your dream? Did that have a positive or a negative effect on your wellbeing? Hope and expectation lead to ambition and achievement. It would be wrong to suggest that we should not have ambition. After all, only by ignoring the naysayers and proving critics wrong have people achieved the greatest things.

And yet there is something about the setting of realistic expectations that enables the mind to focus on other things. We have often seen people spend time understanding their objectives and motivations and come to terms with their realistic goals. Once these have been set, the person can focus on what is in front of them, often the smaller things in life.

CONCLUSION

Having options contributes to financial wellbeing. Increased wealth allows for more options, which is a good reason for embarking on a financial plan. But there are also other ways to create more options.

PART SIX

GETTING YOUR AFFAIRS IN ORDER

In order to use our wealth and maximise wellbeing, we have discussed creating a financial plan, setting up protection from financial shocks, and challenged some of our assumptions to create more options. We can now consider one more area to enhance our financial wellbeing: ensuring security for those we leave behind. The general principle is to prepare for the worst and hope for the best.

NEW LIFE, MID-LIFE OR LIFE-THREATENING

This section is relevant to everyone, but will be more meaningful to some. It focuses on the financial aspects of getting your affairs in order, but will inevitably touch upon more personal outcomes. Having a tidy life at a difficult time will boost your wellbeing. This is true whether starting a family, experiencing the confusion of mid-life changes, or if suffering a life-threatening illness. All of these are difficult times and bring with them worries and responsibilities for others.

REDUCING STRESS

Increasing wellbeing and reducing stress are like considering whether the glass is half full or half empty. It doesn't actually make any difference – all that matters is that you have half a glass! For those suffering a life-threatening illness, not having your affairs in order can be a major source of stress. Taking only a few small steps to address this can make a significant difference to your wellbeing.

Whatever your stress level, if you do all of the following your wellbeing should be considerably enhanced by a reduction in worry. Let's look at some of the ways you can get your affairs in order.

THE FAMILY CONSTITUTION

It might seem that the first place to start would be practical suggestions relating to paperwork. In fact, one of the biggest causes of stress can be worry that your wishes are not fully understood by the ones you leave behind. A family constitution is therefore a very formal way of communicating your wishes and principles. This can be particularly important when there are business interests involved.

STRUCTURE

Like a will, a family constitution is simply a written summary of your wishes. As such, it can take any form, although it will almost always be a formal document drawn up by a solicitor. Typically it will establish a set of core principles for the family and bind adherence to those principles with regard to the family wealth or business. However, the term could equally be used for something much simpler, for example the desire for a family heirloom to always be kept in the family.

A family constitution is not legally binding. However, if it is written in conjunction with business interests or other legal instruments such as trusts (see below), it is possible to ensure your wishes and principles are set firmly for the future.

THE FAMILY MEETING

As with many other types of plans, it is not just the finished document that is useful. The process of discussion and coming to a final set of principles and instructions is often where much of the benefit lies. It is a good idea to use a third party to chair such a meeting – perhaps a family friend or, even better, a professional who knows you well (solicitor, financial planner, accountant).

The objective of this meeting is two-fold: first, it aims to set out your wishes and desires. Second, it provides an opportunity for your family members and loved ones to understand and accept these wishes. After all, they are the ones who are going to have to carry them out when you are gone. Further meetings may well be necessary, depending on the complexity of the issues, perhaps individually and maybe a final review meeting before the solicitor drafts the constitution itself.

WHAT GOES IN A FAMILY CONSTITUTION?

There could be an almost infinite number of examples of these, but we'll pick two. Perhaps Mum has a piece of jewellery and some medals that were handed down to her by her father. She wants these to stay in the family and they must never be sold. Communicating these wishes to her children and grandchildren would give Mum considerable wellbeing–and having them written down even more so.

A far more complicated situation could be a family business, where the shares are spread among three or four siblings. A much more comprehensive document that sets out the principles and ethics of the business will be required. In effect, this provides a mission statement for the family and can even include penalties for non-compliance.

THE WILL

Everyone should have written a will. No exceptions – that includes you. At its very basic level, a will outlines clear instructions on the distribution of your property and possessions. It can do so much more, including tax planning and what should happen to minor children in the event of death. This is particularly useful when there are children from a previous relationship.

A will can save a lot of heartache for those left behind. It can save a lot of money in the long run, not only in taxes but also in legal fees. Sorting out a badly worded homemade will or an argument between beneficiaries can be very costly.

Anyone who has children under 18 should consider a will compulsory. Although the appointment of guardians does not have to be part of a will, it is an obvious place for it. By appointing guardianship through a will, parents can provide clear instructions. Without this inclusion, you are leaving it to a court to decide the fate of your children. You should not leave the decision on how your estate should benefit your children to the vagaries of the statutory rules – you may be doing them no favour in allowing them to inherit a large sum at age 18. Even if your children are over 18, there may be good reason why a trust would be suitable until they have shown themselves to be sensible with money.

If you do not have a will, the law will dictate how your estate is dispersed. This has led to difficult situations and arguments that can break up families. So if you haven't got a will, go and see a solicitor today. Right now. Put this book down, pick up the telephone, and make an appointment. Go on!

If you have made a will but it hasn't been reviewed either for ten years or if your assets or life have changed since, then that applies to you too!

Good, now you've done that we can move on.

ONLINE/HOMEMADE WILLS

It is possible to download a will off the internet and save yourself a few quid. You can also get a do-it-yourself pack from various stationers. Either of these may well turn out to be a false economy. In particular, be wary of free will-writing services. In some cases the writer may put themselves in as executor and will then charge a handsome fee for administering your estate after your death.

THE ONE ABOUT WRITING YOUR OWN WILL

Tom had been a businessman running a small company before he retired, so he felt more than capable of drawing up a "simple" will. He had never been married, had no children, and his closest family included a nephew and two great-nieces that he rarely saw. He wrote a will leaving £20,000 to each of his great-nieces once they reached 25, to help them buy a house. He then divided the rest of his estate between 20 beneficiaries – a mix of charities, friends, and family.

When he died 15 years later, his two great-nieces were aged 19 and 21. The will that Tom wrote did not specify that income from the £20,000 that accumulated over the years should be added to the £20,000 and passed to his great-nieces. This meant that the income belonged to the other 20 beneficiaries. The amount that the great-nieces received would have been around £41,000, but they only received the original £20,000 as stated in the will. Not enough for a deposit on a house. To further complicate matters, Tom did not include the correct wording after his signature. The court ask for the witnesses on the will to be traced so that they could to confirm their actions as witnesses. This delayed the settling of the will by many months.

As with financial planning, we strongly recommend that you obtain advice from an expert when it comes to writing your will. You should also note that a will is void if your marital status changes.

EXECUTOR

The executor of your will is the person who will carry out your wishes as outlined in that document. Choosing this person is, therefore, extremely important. Even if you do not think you have anything to leave to survivors, it is worth having a will simply to name an executor. This will give someone authority to act in dealing with your estate (without this only the court can give that authority) and means you get to choose the person best able to carry out the job. There will still be things to get in order, however little you own. The person the state chooses for the role won't necessarily be the one you think is best.

The ideal person is going to be someone you are close to, but perhaps not so close that they find the task emotionally difficult. Most importantly, it will be someone who is very good at administration and paperwork and has some understanding of financial and tax matters. Make all parties aware of your choice of executor, including your family but also your professional advisers, especially your solicitor and financial planner.

TIP: If you are appointing your solicitor to act as executor, make sure you clarify fees beforehand. Be particularly wary of appointing an institution such as a bank as your executor. Fees for undertaking the task of executor can be astronomical. Always check the details for proposed fees. Although in principle an executor can be asked to step down and may agree not to act, each institution or firm will have a different policy if asked to step down. The last thing your nearest and dearest will want is to be arguing about this at such a painful time. If you appoint a family member or friend as executor, they can always appoint a solicitor to help deal with the administration.

It may be wise for your executor to have a short meeting with a solicitor so that he or she can help assess whether the fees would be worthwhile. Depending on the complexity of the estate, the solicitor would probably know a lot more about the tax savings that can be made during the administration – income tax and capital gains tax, as well as the obvious one, inheritance tax.

It's a good idea to involve your loved ones in the process of writing the will. There is no reason why the reading of the will should be a stressful moment for anyone – let's leave such dramatic moments to the old Agatha Christie novels where they belong! The will becomes a public document once a grant of probate has been issued, in any event. The only caveat would be if you think you may change your will in a few years time and involving the family now could backfire!

FUNERAL WISHES

Although these particular wishes are not binding on your executors, setting down in black and white what you would like takes a weight off the minds of those organising your funeral. Odd though it may seem, disagreements between family members about the funeral do arise and can make a painful time even more anguished. If you do not want to include this in your will, you can leave a side letter of wishes. Store it with your will or somewhere you know it will be found soon after your death.

TIDY UP

Take some time to go through your paperwork. Even better, sit down with someone and let them know what you have and where things are. Make a note of daily tasks that only you know how to do, such as how to set the timer on the central heating, and things like passwords to online accounts. Astonishingly, many grieving spouses don't claim a life assurance policy because they didn't know it existed.

TIP: Create a list or a simple spreadsheet of your assets and insurance policies, including policy numbers and providers (or ask your financial planner for such a list). Give this list to your executor or store it with your will. Update it every time you make a change.

Make a list of logins and passwords for your online accounts: do not give this list to your executor but tell them of its existence. Put the list in a sealed envelope and store it securely. Again, update the list regularly.

If important documents are referenced, such as title deeds to a house or trust deeds, then make a note of where they are kept. And don't forget to include the whereabouts of these in your will!

INTRODUCE YOUR ADVISERS TO YOUR FAMILY

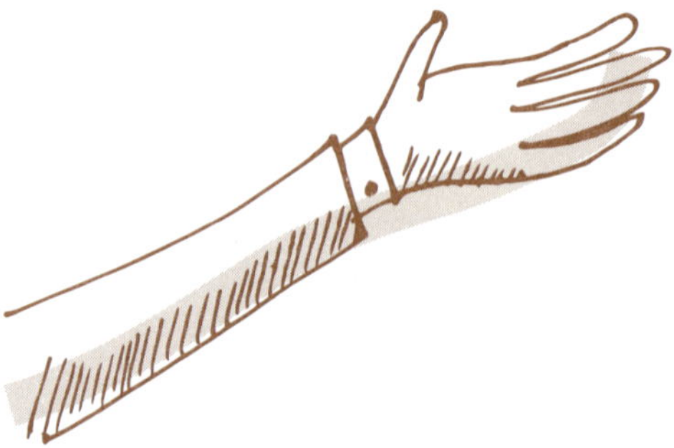

Whether you are suffering from an illness or just thinking about life after you pass, it is a good idea to introduce your family to your advisers. Not only will you be able to make your wishes clear to all parties, but there will be comfort in knowing that the good advice you received will continue to be offered to your loved ones.

It is not uncommon for one partner in a relationship to be the one that deals with the finances. If this partner passes away, the grief and panic that the surviving partner feels is significantly increased by a lack of understanding about the finances managed by the other.

How we manage our affairs can easily continue to affect the wellbeing of our loved ones after we are gone.

THE ONE ABOUT DAD BEING TOO CAREFUL

Mike and Sandra had been married for 40 years. Mike always handled the financial matters, paying the bills, setting budgets, and so on. When Mike retired with a good income and a large cash sum from his pension, he allowed them both one holiday a year to Devon. He took on the task of managing their investments, something that kept him busy in retirement.

Mike died five years later. On top of the grief of losing her husband, Sandra was plunged into panic at having to deal with daily bills and the banking, let alone looking after the investment portfolios. Sandra asked their two daughters to help, who in turn engaged us. We discovered Mike had built up a sizeable investment portfolio. This, along with the house (which was much too big for just Sandra) and the pension income, meant that Sandra was a rather wealthy woman. Rather than being happy at this news, Sandra was actually very angry. In her view, she and Mike could have had a much more active lifestyle in their last five years together. She had wanted to travel, but Mike had said they could only afford the one holiday a year. It seemed he was so determined to leave Sandra and the girls well off that he forgot to spend money on creating memories while he was with them.

TRUSTS—SEPARATING OWNERSHIP INTO ACCESS AND CONTROL

There are two characteristics of owning something:

- The right to benefit from it – access
- The right to decide who benefits from it – control.

A trust can be used to separate these two features.

There can be many reasons why people would choose to separate the access and control of an investment. One common reason is that by giving up control, the asset can be removed from their estate for inheritance tax purposes, and yet they can continue to act as a trustee and decide who should be given the benefits from the asset.

Another typical scenario is when a trust is used to put conditions on who can benefit from an asset. For example, a sum of money could be placed in a trust where it is specified that the sums are to be forwarded only for the income and maintenance of grandchildren (for example, school fees). The money then stays within the trust until each child reaches a certain age, typically 25, when they are allowed to take out their share.

The use of trusts is a speciality area of financial planning and law and therefore requires expert advice.

MENTAL CAPACITY

It might be that you have an illness that will make it difficult for you to manage your own finances or make decisions in the future. Or it may be that you are just worried about such an eventuality, for example, in the event of a stroke. Wellbeing comes from removing worry, so this is an important issue to sort out.

A power of attorney is a way of handing over control of your finances to another person (typically a family member or close friend). It only comes into force when it is needed, so it acts as a safety net without worry about losing control – it will come into force only in the extreme circumstance that you no longer have control anyway. A power of attorney can cover finances and/or health issues and is an extremely useful way to ensure that you will continue to be looked after in the event of your incapacitation.

Again, this is an important legal document and specialist advice should be obtained. In the meantime, there is a good information on this subject on the Macmillian Cancer Support website: http://www.macmillan.org.uk/.

LONG-TERM CARE

There are very specific rules around the funding of long-term care fees, particularly surrounding property. It is best to get such issues understood and decided upon long before they become essential. Not all financial planners specialise in this area, so make sure you speak to an adviser who has the suitable knowledge and experience to be able to advise you.

FUNERAL ARRANGEMENTS

I don't know about you, but I want there to be a party when I go.

Let there be tears, let there be moments of sadness, but I'd like to be celebrated with a twinkle in the eye and a laugh about the good times. I've already picked the song I want to be cremated to and told my kids where I want the ashes scattered.

There is peace of mind from discussing such issues with your loved ones, especially knowing that there will be fewer decisions to be made in those difficult days following your passing, whenever that may be. And with peace of mind comes wellbeing.

CONCLUSION

Like a spring cleaning, the process of getting one's affairs in order can be daunting and off-putting; however, there is wellbeing to be had once the job is done. Sorting out the paperwork, leaving clear instructions on where things are, discussing and communicating your desires for how assets should be used after you are gone, and handing over control to others all contribute to our wellbeing. Once done, these actions remove the clutter from our minds and clear the way for more important thoughts and concerns, a process which in itself gives financial wellbeing.

PART **SEVEN**

HOW YOUR **FINANCIAL WELLBEING** AFFECTS OTHER AREAS OF **WELLBEING**

Financial wellbeing is just one of five areas of wellbeing: career wellbeing, social wellbeing, physical wellbeing, community wellbeing, and of course financial wellbeing. None of these operate in isolation.

Now that we have been through the different aspects of financial wellbeing, we will consider the other areas of wellbeing in turn. How do the changes you have made to enhance your financial wellbeing affect the other four areas, and is there anything more that you can do?

CAREER WELLBEING

A word that is a useful measure of career wellbeing is how **engaged** a person is. People who are engaged in their daily life are likely to get fulfilment from their work. Often their work may spill over into their daily lives.

When we meet in a social situation, a common question we ask in order to get the measure of each other is, "What do you do for a living?"

TIP: When you meet someone at a party, trying asking a question that is not related to that person's work. For example, try, "Hi Bob, nice to meet you. Tell me, what makes you happy?"

This area is tied to our sense of purpose. The more engaged we are, the greater sense of purpose we have, and the higher our career wellbeing. But how does this link with financial wellbeing? And what could employers learn about wellbeing in the workplace?

THE ONE ABOUT THE MAN WITH MONEY AND THE MAN WITH A JOB

Courtney is a client in addition to being a personal friend. He had sold his business a few years previously and had cash in the bank. He was involved in a charity and as a governor at his local school, but was looking for a new challenge. He was a bit bored.

A week later I was talking with Syd, another client who is also a friend. He had been at the helm of this family business for some 20 years and was frustrated that all his wealth was tied up in the company. If he could release cash by selling the business, he felt, then he would have more options.

I told Syd about Courtney. Maybe he could sell his business to Courtney? Perhaps they should meet and talk it over. I told Courtney about Syd's business. He was very interested. A week later, having not heard from Syd, I gave him a call. What did he think? Would he like to speak to Courtney about selling the business? Syd said he'd been thinking about it, and decided not to sell after all.

"What brought about this change in thinking?" I asked.

"Because," Syd replied, "if I sold my business to Courtney, we'd just swap places. I'd be a guy with cash and nothing to do, and he'd be a guy with a business that frustrated him."

Instead, Syd engaged a business coach and went about changing his own role in the business so that he would be more engaged. At the time of writing he is still running his business and can't imagine ever not doing so.

Clearly there is a link between financial wellbeing and career wellbeing. We have to work at a job to pay the bills and provide the savings that generate wealth. Sometimes being engaged and having a sense of purpose can feel like a luxury. Follow the process of "know thyself". Spend time understanding what aspects of your work you find engaging. If you are able to, arrange your role so that you spend more time doing those things.

By making the changes to your financial position outlined in this book, you should have more options and action points to align your life with your expectations. In some cases, maybe expectations changed to become aligned with your financial position. If you can't get a better-paying job, sell your business, or ask your boss for a raise, then try to organise your role to do more of what you enjoy.

And if all that doesn't work, then it might just be necessary to change your attitude!

THE ONE ABOUT JOHN BRACEWELL

John Bracewell (real name!) was the head coach for Gloucestershire County Cricket Club in 1998. They had never won a trophy in their 100+ year history. John changed the mindset of the club and not only did they win their first trophy, but went on to dominate cricket in England for the next five years, winning a total of nine trophies.

I was a trainee cricket coach doing my level-two qualification and John had been invited to talk to our group. One point he made in particular has always stuck with me. Some fielding positions are more important than others on a cricket pitch. Fine leg, for example, which is behind the wicket keeper, can be a bit dull, seeing little of the action. Often bowlers field in that position so that they can have a rest.

John made the point that every position on a field is crucial and that all players must always give their best for the team at all times. If you are asked to field at fine leg, he said, then you must try and be the very best fine leg that you can possibly be.

I always thought that was wise advice and highly applicable to the workplace and beyond. It certainly worked for Gloucestershire CCC.

WELLBEING IN THE WORKPLACE – A WORD FOR EMPLOYERS

A lot of wellbeing in the workplace is driven by human resources departments, and tends to focus on support. This might mean debt counselling, or providing information on the company pension scheme. These tend to focus on the negative, such as giving up smoking or reducing alcohol intake. There is a lot that can be done to promote positive wellbeing; a few examples are given above.

Such positive steps should be offered alongside financial education. However, be careful about who you invite to talk to your employees. In order to maximise the wellbeing from financial education in the workplace, the advice should be focused on planning, and for maximum wellbeing should start with coaching (see page 142 for more details).

WELLBEING IN THE WORKPLACE – CAREER

The financial plan that will be emerging from working through this book should give clarity to what the future might look like and how it will be funded. How much more powerful could this plan be if it was aligned with a career path?

Many employers have an appraisal structure with staging posts and a long-term career strategy. If this were produced in conjunction with a financial plan, which may even show the life changes possible by promotion or bonuses available, the effect on wellbeing could be considerable.

WELLBEING IN THE WORKPLACE – WORKPLACE PENSIONS

A good example of potential wellbeing is how employers implement staff pension schemes. We have seen that wellbeing stems from having a clear path to achievable objectives. A major plank of having a clear path is savings. Workplace pensions should therefore be seen as a key employee benefit.

Too often, however, employees view their pension scheme with mistrust.

THE ONE ABOUT A NEW STAFF PENSION SCHEME

Arthur and I were in the pub one evening. He pulled out a piece of paper and asked me to take a look. It was about his company's pension scheme. It seemed the company was changing the provider for the second time in as many years. Arthur said staff were very unhappy about the change and believed the company were trying to profit by the change. What did I think?

He had given me the announcement email from the company. It contained jargon that I understood, but Arthur could not. In essence it announced that the pension was being moved to a new employer so that they could get more information about the scheme easily online ("flexible benefits") and reduce the cost ("on-going management charges"). Far from being a bad thing, the company was making a change that was very much in the employees' interest. Because the company had not engaged the staff but just sent out an email filled with confusing terms, the result was a decrease in wellbeing, rather than an increase.

In order for staff to appreciate the benefit they get from workplace pensions, they need to understand their own long-term motivations. In this way they will create expectations and objectives, which the pension scheme can help to meet.

WELLBEING IN THE WORKPLACE – OTHER BENEFITS AT WORK

Some companies offer other benefits for employees, such as life assurance or private medical insurance. However, it is important that employees understand and appreciate what they have as part of their package for wellbeing to follow, and for the company to receive any benefit from what it's providing.

A good example of a benefit with strong financial wellbeing is the "Cycle to Work" schemes. This enables staff to buy a bike tax-free and spread the cost. An employer could go one step further and establish a link with a local cycling club.

Employee benefits should be designed to enhance wellbeing. For example, when I was last employed by a large corporation, we had discount cards for use at certain retailers. As we saw on page 54, retail therapy adds little to wellbeing. I would have gained more wellbeing from an extra day's holiday or from participating in experiences.

The total sum of our various connections with other people determines our social wellbeing. We are hugely influenced by others, and if someone we know is happy, then we are more likely to be happy as well. The converse is also true. The concept of poisonous characters in a workplace is well known. One person with a bad attitude can infect a whole group of people. If you are struggling with your own positive attitude, it might be a good idea to stay away from those people who always tend to see the worst in a situation. Indeed, according to research, the effect of our friends' wellbeing on our own is much greater than financial wellbeing. If a direct connection is happy, we are 15% more likely to be happy[14]. An increase in income of £10,000, however, is only likely to increase our happiness by 2%[15].

So if you want to increase wellbeing, make that phone call to the old friend you haven't spoken to for a while. Don't text, e-mail, or Facebook them – actually speak to him or her. Share some good news. Simply having positive relationships reduces stress levels.

SHARING LIFE-THREATENING ILLNESS

Studies have proven that positive relationships actually help the healing process. And yet an illness such as cancer can put tremendous strain on relationships, just at the very time our bodies need those relationships to be strong and positive. It is not uncommon for people undergoing treatment for cancer, for example, to want to keep their illness a secret, often from friends, and sometimes from their own family. This could be because they don't want to worry or frighten people close to them, they don't want to make a fuss, or perhaps they are struggling to come to terms with their illness themselves. And yet studies show that the support and friendship of loved ones can reduce stress and actually aid in the healing process. Once you start talking about your illness, others feel able to as well.

THE ONE ABOUT SIGNING OVER THE CAR

Dave had been diagnosed with cancer and was going through chemotherapy. The future was uncertain and he was struggling to deal with what he was faced with. Among other things, he worried about how his wife, Rosie, was going to cope after he had gone. One day, Dave took the step of putting his car into Rosie's name. He said later that this small act was one of the most healing things that he could have done. It began the process of focusing on himself and his illness and worrying less about others. For Rosie, it was the beginning of them learning to live with Dave's illness.

Not sharing might mean denying those who care about you the opportunity to help.

HELPING OTHERS

As we considered in the section on philanthropy (page 58), helping others can bring about enormous wellbeing. It is where social wellbeing and financial wellbeing meet, and help and support can come from giving of time as well as money

THE ONE ABOUT MY GRANDMOTHER

My grandmother was four feet and a couple of peanuts tall, and a ball of energy. We would go round for tea every other Sunday and nothing was ever too much bother for her. She used to help out with day trips for the local old people's homes. She would push wheelchairs and help people – most of them in their 70s and 80s – on and off the coaches. My father would sometimes question this, worried that she was doing too much.

"Oh, don't fuss," she would reply. "I just like to help out the old people."

She was 82 at the time.

MONEY AND SOCIAL WELLBEING

One of the biggest forms of negative social relationships is peer pressure. It is common to judge one's own success by reference to those around us. The concept of "know thyself" is perhaps as relevant here as in any other area. However well-off we are is entirely related to how well-off we need to be in order to achieve our objectives and motivations in life. It has no bearing whatsoever on how well-off our friends are. And yet this social context of our wealth is the standard by which we judge our success.

TIP: Follow the steps outlined in this book and you will have plotted a path to *your* financial wellbeing. This act in itself will make you less inclined to compare your wealth with your peers, which will enhance your social wellbeing and therefore your overall wellbeing.

PHYSICAL WELLBEING

Food is the fuel to our body. The better the quality of the food, the better our body's ability to be healthy. A healthy body is better equipped to fight disease because it nurtures the immune system. Being fit and healthy is clearly a good thing to be.

So is there a relationship between good financial planning and food? Not necessarily. Your level of wealth is not linked to whether you can eat healthily or exercise regularly. And yet it is true to say that the lower-paid tend to eat less healthily[16]. The irony is that eating poorly, whether it is ready-made meals or junk food, is often more expensive than cooking fresh food. *It doesn't cost anything to go out for a run or exercise at home.*

COMMUNITY WELLBEING

We are social animals. Take our living patterns, for example. We choose to gather in cities, squeezing together and happily getting on each other's nerves! Why are we not evenly spread across the planet, each person having a similar size home on a few acres of land? The fact that we gather together makes it logical that our level of wellbeing increases with the extent and quality of our social interactions. However, this needs to be the appropriate interaction for you. More than one person has moved to an idyllic cottage in the country only to be bored and lonely. Wellbeing will increase depending upon issues such as proximity to family (probably close, but in some instances as far away as possible!).

A survey[17] found that the three main aspects of a community that made it a place where people liked to live were: opportunities for social engagement (bars, restaurants, entertainment); acceptance of others; aesthetics (availability of parks, if the community is in a beautiful setting).

They also found that community wellbeing increased with education and wealth. That's hardly surprising – those with more wealth are able to afford the nicer parts of town. But wealth is not required for openness or engaging in community activities that bring social engagement.

On page 56 we saw that buying experiences contributed far more to wellbeing than the accumulation of wealth. How we spend our money on a daily basis adds more to wellbeing than the ownership of money itself. A key relationship between financial and community wellbeing, therefore, is not so much how we spend our money, but how we spend our time. Bearing this in mind, the ideal combination for enhancing wellbeing would be to use our wealth to create free time, which we then use to give back to our communities.

THE ONE ABOUT THE IDEAL WORK-LIFE BALANCE

Jack had worked hard for ten years building his small business. During that time he had put some of his profits into a pension plan and paid off his mortgage. At the age of 45 Jack sold his business. The amount he received wasn't enough to retire but, with the pension, he did have options. He was married with two children, aged seven and nine.

Before completing the sale Jack came to see us to work out how much he needed to sell the business for. We prepared a cash-flow forecast based on a sum that would provide Jack with enough to retire at 60, but still working and earning in the interim.

Jack had decided he would split his week as follows:

- Three days working (initially consulting, until one of his old clients offered him a job)
- One day on charity (he offered himself as a trustee to a local charity that snapped him up)
- One day on community (as a governor in his children's school)

Working three days gave him enough income to live on. On the other two days he took his children to school and then took great satisfaction from being able to give something back. A combination of the financial planning, choosing to spend his money by working less, and how he spent that spare time resulted in a huge increase in Jack's wellbeing.

PART EIGHT

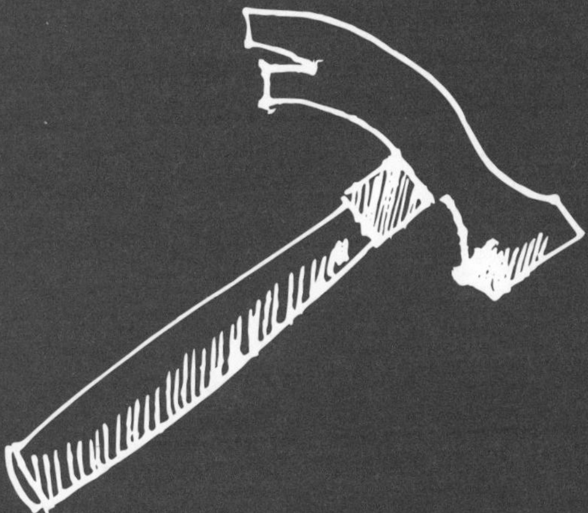

TAKING ADVICE OR DOING IT YOURSELF

"If you think it's expensive to hire a professional to do the job, wait until you hire an amateur." - Red Adair

You might think that, as a financial planner myself, I would be biased on the subject of seeking professional advice or managing your own financial planning and investments. In the spirit of "know thyself", I am actually all for the do-it-yourself approach – for the right person. My support of DIY investing, therefore, comes with a big caveat, a golden rule: only do something you know how to do.

DIY is a good metaphor for managing your own investments. As a person who could not even hang a mirror the right way, I wouldn't dream of doing anything more to my house than changing a light bulb (and even then only after reading the instructions).

Hiring a financial planner should add value. What you should not do, I believe, is to judge the advice you receive based solely on how much it costs. When it comes to financial planning and managing investments, therefore, I would suggest you either:

- Do it yourself if you are knowledgeable and have the time to do so

or

- Engage a financial planner.

Let's look at these two approaches and determine which is most likely to increase *your* financial wellbeing.

DOING IT YOURSELF

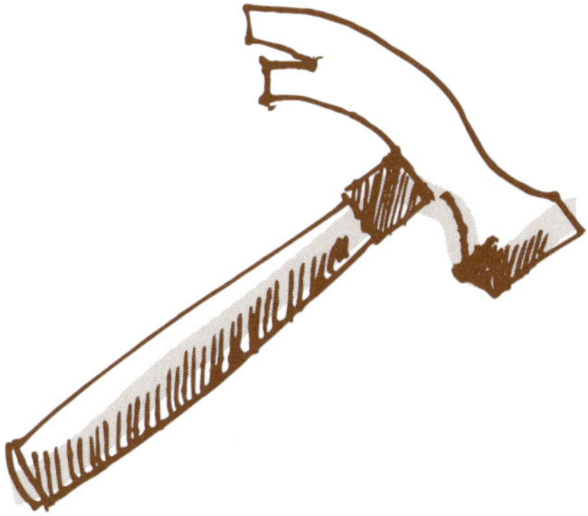

The aim of this book has been to encourage you to find a clearer picture of your future, and then to create a clear path to help you achieve those goals and objectives. When it comes to managing the investments to help you get there, it may therefore be that you only require information.

Many websites provide information for people who want to make financial planning and investment decisions without necessarily seeing a financial planner, such as BoringMoney.co.uk. The use of such an alternative to a financial planner may be because such individuals have experience and knowledge, or because the sum of money in question is not really big enough to justify the fees of a financial planner. An example of this could be setting up a junior ISA for the kids. If you have £3,000 to save this way, for example, paying an hourly fee for advice is not going to be viable. Many financial planners do not take on clients with smaller pots of money to invest, due to regulatory and other costs.

DIY OPTIONS FOR INVESTMENTS

If you want to stick a toe into the investment waters, whether it is to save into an ISA or even to start a DIY personal pension (a Self-Invested Personal Pension or SIPP for short), help is available online. Your best bet is to look at what is called an investment platform. Think of this like a financial department store, a one-stop shop for all your investment needs. Financial planning websites rate and review various service providers online, taking into account service and cost. There are also regular features in the personal finance sections of newspapers such as the *Mail on Sunday*, *The Times* and *The Telegraph* that cover this subject.

The platforms reviewed make a lot of sense for the DIY investor since all investments, including ISAs and SIPPs, can be held in a single account. Most of them will also allow access to a range of the world's best fund managers, as well as providing a share-trading service. They are convenient and typically decently priced compared to some of the more opaque structures cooked up by the financial services industry in the past.

DIY COSTS

As a rule of thumb, you should expect to pay:

- Between 0.25%–0.45% for the "shop" (that's the platform fee, which will normally include all ISA charges)
- About 0.65%–0.75% to the fund manager, who manages any funds you choose
- About £10 to buy or sell a share, and
- There will be extra charges if you are setting up a SIPP.

A typical ISA investor, for example, might expect to pay between £100 and £120 for every £10,000 invested in an ISA on the platform. That's between 1% and 1.2% all-in for the "shop" and the products on the shelves. Obviously there is no fee for financial planning or tax advice because you're not getting any!

HELP WITH CHOOSING FUNDS

Although many of these platforms will provide tips and pointers about investments, they will not give you tailored advice specific to your needs or help with anything other than which funds to pick. Look for their fund shortlists, or preferred lists, which will guide you to a much narrower list of investments to choose from, usually banded into different risk categories.

ROBO ADVICE

Another development is the rather strangely named "Robo Advice". These are online investment services that typically ask investors a range of questions to ascertain their attitude to investment risk. Once this has been established, investors are then allocated a basket of investments deemed suitable for that level of risk. They are strangely named because they don't actually give advice. A more appropriate term would be "automated investment portfolios".

This service will appeal to those who do not have the confidence to pick the actual investments (funds and shares) that go into a portfolio. It's the financial equivalent of buying a ready-meal instead of a list of ingredients. These services will typically make use of low-cost "passive" funds and the all-in cost will be in the region of 0.75%–1.2%.

PENSIONS

It is important to take into account tax when investing, and pensions and ISAs are the two most commonly used tax vehicles for investments. Many platforms offer SIPPs (Self-Invested Personal Pensions), which are an attractive way to start saving for your retirement and supplement any workplace pension you might have. As we have seen, the earlier you start to save the better, and some platforms will let you start with a monthly direct debit commitment of £25.

AT RETIREMENT

DIY platforms are a sensible way to start a retirement savings pot. However, when it comes to drawing a pension and deciding what to do at the point of retirement, it would advisable to invest in financial advice, as this can become horribly complicated.

TIP: Remember – financial planning and investment management are not the same thing. All of the above services only offer investment management.

SOME BASIC INVESTMENT RULES

Investing can seem a little like gambling. Some people say they have a fool-proof system, some invest using technical analysis, some use their gut feelings, and others are scared off by the very idea of investing. Here are a few basic rules to remember, some of which reiterate points already made:

- The ideal investment is one that goes up at a higher rate than inflation but can't go down
- Such an investment simply cannot exist, by the laws of economics. If it did, everyone would invest in it and inflation would increase
- The general public more often than not invests emotionally. They

tend to go in at the top of a market (when they feel confident), and get out at the bottom (when they panic)

- An individual's risk tolerance tends to remain stable over time
- An individual's perception of risk tends to change over time, and is often followed by an emotional asset purchase or sale decision
- Past performance of investments is not necessarily a guide to their future performance
- It's always a good idea to spread a portfolio around a variety of investments to reduce the effect of one of the investments failing
- Many people get very interested in buying shares but do not continue to monitor performance and reassess their holdings on a regular basis. It is important to assess the future potential of an investment on a regular basis.
- The classic comment made by the American financier Bernard Baruch: "Nobody ever lost money taking a profit."
- There is no such thing as a sure-fire winner or a quick buck. And the old adage, "If it looks too good to be true it probably is", was never more appropriate than when applied to investing.

DON'T FORGET THE TAX

Using current tax rules can make an enormous difference to wealth creation and investment returns. Whether it is using pensions for tax relief, ISAs for tax-free growth, or taking profit to use the capital gains tax allowance, make sure you have a basic working knowledge of the current tax rules.

The purpose of this book is *not* to teach you how to be an investment expert. The aim of this book is to improve your financial wellbeing. That requires a better understanding of yourself and aligning your finances accordingly.

YOU CAN'T CHALLENGE YOURSELF

DIY investing may well be ideal for you. Perhaps you have been able to use this book to put in place a clear path to identifiable objectives, and can now manage your own investments to those objectives. The one thing you will never be able to do, however, is to challenge your own assumptions. It is for this reason that I engage a financial planner myself. I pay someone to help map out my family's financial future, to challenge my assumptions, and to dare me to dream. It gives me peace of mind to know someone will be there to help look after things if anything were to happen to me.

Paying a financial planner gives *me* wellbeing.

USING A FINANCIAL ADVISER

HOW FINANCIAL PLANNERS INCREASE WELLBEING

A survey[18] looked at things that people liked to do the least. It appears that the second least desirable daily activity is financial/ government services, second only to personal medical care. It seems we would rather do homework, wash dishes, or even do the ironing than spend time working out our finances!

WHAT TYPE OF ADVISER DO YOU NEED?

As with any other type of advice, there are many ways to receive financial advice. Whichever you choose, make sure they are authorised and regulated by the Financial Conduct Authority (FCA). You can do this by checking the register at www.fca.org.uk. Some scammers claim to be regulated but they are not and the FCA website lists all reputable advisors.

There are three stages to true financial planning, and these should be followed in order. Some firms will do one, some will do two, and some will do all three.

These are, in order:

1. Coaching – helping you understand yourself by creating and discovering objectives
2. Planning – mapping a path to those objectives
3. Advising – using products to direct you along the path to your objectives.

At the basic level, a financial adviser will assess your circumstances and provide *advice* as to what products they think you need that are most suitable for your requirements. Alternatively, some financial planners can map out your financial future. They will ask for your objectives and plan a path toward your desired outcomes and then monitor your progress. Only once the *planning* has been done, will they move to the *advice* stage and recommend products to help achieve the plan. A growing number of firms can provide *coaching* to help you work out your objectives before moving onto the *planning* and *advice* stages. They will challenge and dare you to dream in order to create a financial plan that is truly meaningful.

When receiving financial advice, it is important to understand the difference between these three approaches. If you have had experience with bad advice in the past, it may be because you didn't take advice from a firm or an individual that provided the type of advice you needed.

Note: Another term you may come across is wealth manager. Wealth managers are typically for investments only and do not provide financial advice or planning. Some larger firms will have several departments offering several of these different services.

WHAT DOES A GOOD FINANCIAL ADVISER FIRM LOOK LIKE?

The answer to this question can only come back to the same question: what sort of advice do you need? If you have a limited budget or have a need for a specific product (for example, someone with young children wanting to take out life assurance), then a one-off product advice may be sufficient.

In this case the cost of the advice is going to be important. Advisers should make the costs clear at the outset, whether they are paid by commission or by a fee. Since 2013, they will only be able to take a commission for arranging insurance or mortgage products, but that doesn't stop you from asking for a fee-based service even for these areas. You may also want to check if they are able to recommend a product from the whole of the market or have a limited range of products from which to select. If you require planning or coaching-based advice, then your needs are likely to be both more complex and ongoing.

When assessing firms to help you with financial planning, you may wish to consider the following factors:

- Do they offer a free initial meeting for you to decide if you want to use them (and for them to decide if they want to work with you)?
- Are their charges clear and understandable? Price might not be the most important factor when selecting a firm to help you, but you should understand at an early stage what the costs are likely to be, typically after the initial telephone call or meeting.
- Do they have a robust process for providing reviews (annual should suffice, possibly twice yearly if you feel it would add value)?
- Do they have a broad range of technical knowledge? This does not have to be all from one individual. For example, some firms will have a pensions specialist or may outsource such work.
- If you require help in working out what your future might look like, do the advisers have training in coaching skills?
- Do you like them?

FINDING AN ADVISER

The most common way of finding someone to help you with your finances is through a recommendation. However, recommendations shouldn't be the sole basis for making a choice. For example, just because old Joe has been advising your uncle for 20 years doesn't mean he is going to be right for you. The above factors are still important.

TIP: Ask people you respect who they use for financial advice – perhaps a parent, senior manager, or your boss. Ask what they get from their adviser, both in terms of the areas of advice and specific outcomes. Ask if their wellbeing has increased as a result of engaging that adviser.

There are websites that can help you find an adviser, although these do not always accurately filter down to the right one for you, so you will still need to shop around a little.

CONCLUSION

The type of adviser that is right for you, or if you need an adviser at all, will depend upon whether you feel you need one, two, or all three stages of financial advice, coupled with your level of financial knowledge and spare time.

PART NINE

A FINAL WORD

The underlying theme of this book has been "know thyself". Once you know what you want from life, you are better placed to make wise choices. Once you understand what makes you happy and organise your finances around that motivation, you will improve your financial wellbeing.

A RECAP

Throughout this book we have considered the five elements that make up financial wellbeing. Having a clear idea of each of these will create the space for you to make the right decision for yourself. These are:

- A clear path to achieve identifiable objectives
- Control of daily finances
- The ability to cope with a financial shock
- Financial options in life
- Clarity and security for those we leave behind.

Our objective has been to create a financial plan based on the following steps:

STEP 1 Understand your objectives and motivations in life ("know thyself")
STEP 2 Create a realistic financial plan that helps achieve those objectives and motivations
STEP 3 Monitor and review regularly.

Dipping into the book can help improve wellbeing, as doing something is always going to be better than doing *nothing*. However, the effect on wellbeing from completing the whole plan is likely to be greater than the sum of its parts. Don't feel you have completed Step Two (the 'know thyself' part of this process) too soon. Your financial plan should be designed to give you the lifestyle you have chosen, based upon expectations that have been influenced by your finances and earning capacity. This circular logic should be regularly tested until a balance evolves between aspirations, dreams, and the financial reality.

WHAT NEXT?

In some ways, producing the financial plan means you have reached the beginning. A financial plan is never finished. It needs to be refined and changed just as life changes. Your plan should be reviewed at least annually or at major life events. Update values and income, check expenditure assumptions, and re-examine objectives. If you were to go back to the beginning of the book and start again, would the plan that you produced be the same as first time round? If you think the answer is "no," then back you go!

If you are now settled on a financial plan, with clear objectives and motivations, then the next step is to put it out of your mind until next year and go and enjoy the life you have envisioned!

AND FINALLY ...

I started this book with an anecdote about my own search for wellbeing. I'd like to end with an anecdote that shows that wellbeing

doesn't require a large amount of money. Sometimes the smallest sums can change a life.

THE ONE ABOUT THE LAST SHILLING

Mollie Petrie was born in 1920. She enjoyed a highly successful career as a singing coach and garnered an international reputation sufficient to allow her the freedom of Covent Garden Opera House. In her 90s Mollie told me a story that highlights how a tiny sacrifice can go a very, very long way.

Mollie grew up in a poor family in Newcastle. Her father worked in a munitions factory and, as such, was not allowed to sign up as a soldier in the First World War. To avoid accusations of cowardice, such individuals were given a Tommy's Shilling coin.

When Mollie was a girl, her musical talent was identified and she was offered a scholarship to a special music college. She needed to take a train to the interview. Unfortunately, her mother did not have any money to give her for the fare. Mollie would therefore not be able to get to the interview, and wouldn't go to music college.

Mollie told her mother that she knew where there was one last shilling in the house. It was in her mother's "jewellery box". Her mother had no jewellery, but kept the box anyway. Her mother, very much aware of the purpose of that shilling, said she shouldn't take it.

This was, of course, her father's Tommy's Shilling. When her father got back from work, Mollie rushed up and asked him if it would be all right to use this shilling for the train fare. "Of course it would be all right," said her father. Mollie should have the coin because going to college was important. It was, quite literally, the last shilling her family owned. There were no credit cards, there were no overdrafts, and there was no other money.

Mollie passed the interview, attended music college, and went on to coach many of the world's finest singers. She was even made a Freeman of the City of Newcastle. But only because of that last shilling and the sacrifice of a proud father.

WITH THANKS TO:

A number of people have contributed ideas or tips to this book, so a big thanks to:

Laura Kerby, Dr Catherine Zollman, Gill Theodoreson of Penny Brohn UK

Holly Mackay, founder of www.boringmoney.co.uk

My coaching mentor, Jan Bowen-Nielsen www.quivermanagement.co.uk

My Ovation Finance Ltd colleagues, especially Ian Else, Adrian Kidd, Liz Thomas, Tom Dewey, and Tom Morris

Vanessa Eyre of Meade King solicitors (wills)

Malcolm Emery of Thrings solicitors (family constitutions)

Mike Rapps of Gregg Latchams Ltd solicitors (trusts)

Debbie Kleiner-Gaines of PES (wellbeing in the workplace)

Paul Resnik of Finemetrica (risk tolerance)

Phil Young of Threesixty Services for giving the manuscript a sense check

A note about the personal examples used: every anecdote in this book is based on real events; however, names and details have been changed. Apart from the one about my muzzy head – that's entirely true!

THE LEGAL BIT:

Nothing in this book constitutes financial advice. All examples and figures are examples for illustrative purposes only. You should see a regulated financial adviser for advice specific to your own circumstances.

BIBLIOGRAPHY AND REFERENCES

1. (Page ix) Rath and Harter *Financial Wellbeing—Five Essential Elements* (Gallup Press, 2010)

2. (Page x) The Consumer Financial Protection Bureau identifies four areas of financial wellbeing. "Financial well-being: The goal of financial education" (2015) http://www.consumerfinance.gov/reports/financial-well-being/

3. (Page 10) David A Kolb, *Experiential Learning: Experience as the Source of Learning and Development* (Pearson FT Press, Dec 2014)

4. (Page 17) Brickman, Coates, Janoff-Bulman, "Lottery Winners and Accident Victims: Is Happiness Relative?," *Journal of Personality and Social Psychology* Vol 36, No.8, 917-927 (1978) http://pages.ucsd.edu/~nchristenfeld/Happiness_Readings_files/Class%203%20-%20Brickman%201978.pdf

5. (Page 43) Sing Lin, PhD, For every year we work past 55 we lose two years of life expectancy. Optimum Strategies for Creativity and Longevity http://faculty.kfupm.edu.sa/COE/gutub/English_Misc/Retire1.htm

6. (Page 54) Aknin, Dunn, Norton, "Happiness Runs in a Circular Motion: Evidence for a Positive Feedback Loop between Prosocial Spending and Happiness." Published online (April 24 2011) http://www.people.hbs.edu/mnorton/aknin%20dunn%20norton.pdf

7. (Page 54) Dunn, Aknin, Norton, "Spending Money on Others Promotes Happiness." Undated. http://greatergood.berkeley.edu/images/application_uploads/norton-spendingmoney.pdf

8. (Page 56) Study showing how sad individuals spend more.
Cryder, Lerner, Gross and Dhal, "Misery Is Not Miserly" *Psychological Science* (Dec 2007) http://apps.olin.wustl.edu/faculty/cryder/miseryisnotmiserly.pdf

9. (Page 57) More wellbeing from buying experiences.
Gilovich, T., and Kumar, A. , "We'll Always Have Paris: the Hedonic Payoff from Experiential and Material Investments." *M.P. Zanna and J.M. Olson (Eds.), Advances in Experimental Social Psychology,* (2015). Vol. 51, (pp. 147-187), AESP, UK: Academic Press

10. (Page 59) Amar, Ariely, Ayal, Cryder, Rick, "Winning the Battle but Losing the War: the Psychology of Debt Management." *Journal of Market Research*, Vol XIVIII